Nirad C Chaudhuri, The First Hundred Years

NIRAD C CHAUDHURI, THE FIRST HUNDRED YEARS

A Celebration

Edited by

Swapan Dasgupta

HarperCollins *Publishers* India

HarperCollins *Publishers* India Pvt Ltd
7/16 Ansari Road, Daryaganj, New Delhi 110 002

First Published 1997 by
HarperCollins *Publishers* India
Second impression 1998

ISBN 81-7223-293-4

The Publishers gratefully acknowledge permission to reproduce the following essays:
Khushwant Singh's essay 'Nirad C. Chaudhuri, Scholar Extraordinary' first published in *Not a Nice Man to Know*, Viking Penguin India, 1993
Ian Jack's essay 'The World's Last Englishmen' first published in the *London Observer*, 1987

Typeset in Garamond by FOLIO
G-68, Connaught Circus, New Delhi 110 001

Printed in India by
Gopsons Papers Ltd
A-28, Sector IX
Noida 201 301

CONTENTS

INTRODUCTION

Talking of relics, there are still a handful of Bengalis who attach a great deal of importance to form, appearance and heritage. This invariably casts them as Anglophiles in a society that is still unsure of what it means to be Indian. I confess to being a member of this minusculity as does Aveek Sarkar who, among other things, is one of the publishers of Nirad Chandra Chaudhuri's Bengali writings.

It was in February 1995, I was in agreeable exile in London, a victim of one of those drearily familiar coups in newspapers, and Aveek Babu was visiting the city we both regard as a second home, probably from the day we learnt to play Monopoly. After the usual exchange of political gossip and book talk, the conversation inevitably veered to the one obsession that distinguishes a Bengali from his up-country brethren: food. Actually it was drink we were talking about. Sherry, to be precise. Whereas Aveek Babu saw a certain civilized quality to serving a glass of sherry to a pre-lunch visitor, I, being more of the post-EC generation, saw little virtue in fortified wine when good claret was so readily available. Of course, there was a certain practical element to the discussion. Aveek Babu was keen to find out which biscuit was the best accompaniment to sherry. We were both making wild guesses when Aveek Babu proffered a solution: 'Why don't we ask Nirad Babu?' It somehow seemed the most obvious thing to do.

In the afternoon, Aveek Babu having armed himself with a bottle of champagne from Fortnum and Mason that would come up to Nirad Babu's exacting standards, we drove up to Lathbury Road in North Oxford. It was not my first encounter with the Unknown Indian. In the summer of 1983, when I was up at Nuffield College, I made the grave error of introducing myself to him as 'Swapan' with the North Indian emphasis on the w, rather than as 'Shawpone' as the Bengalis prefer. It was an unconscious lapse and did not please Nirad Babu. I am certain some monstrous generalization of the linguistic disorientation of the modern Bengali youth must have taken shape in his mind as a result of that meeting because, twelve years later, he remembered exactly how I had introduced myself earlier.

Although he was still recovering from the shock of his wife's death a few months earlier, Nirad Babu was still sufficiently excited about the 'small monograph—not more than 300 pages' he was writing on his favourite obsessions: the decline of Western civilization. I wrote about our meeting in my weekly column in *The Indian Express:* 'For someone who loves to travel through the subterranean alleys of classicism, Mr Chaudhuri's thesis is remarkably uncomplicated. The West, he argues, has regressed to where it was in the eighth century A.D., between the final collapse of the Greco-Roman civilization and its subsequent Christian reinvigoration. Nirad Babu is uncertain as to who or what will emerge as the new Saint Augustine, but he has little hesitation in identifying the source of the civilizational AIDS. "All that is pernicious and decadent in the West today . . . emanates from across the Atlantic".'

What I did not write about was that Nirad Babu was delighted with Aveek Babu's choice of champagne and visibly tickled at the query over the right biscuit for sherry. He took us to his dining room and took out a packet of water biscuits. 'This is right with sherry', he pronounced grandly and insisted Aveek Babu took away the packet so that he got it right in future.

This incident, insignificant as it is, tells us a great deal about the antipathy that Nirad Chaudhuri invites among his own countrymen. In England, the hallmark of appropriate dressing is the ability to not attract attention to yourself. To be correct, everything has to be understated. For all his avowed Englishness, Nirad Babu has consciously violated this convention. In Delhi, where he lived until 1970, he was completely incongruous in his Kashmiri Gate surroundings and invited taunts of 'Johnny Walker' from bemused local urchins. It was no different in Oxford which has been his home subsequently. There is a delightful scene in a BBC documentary made in the early 1980s which shows a group of yobbish skinheads attempting a war dance around him as he walks unconcerned in his tweeds and felt hat down Broad Street. In 1955, when the Nehru Centre in London invited him for a talk, Nirad Babu startled the expatriate Indian audience by turning up in the ceremonial regalia of a Commander of the British Empire. Earlier, in 1984, I recall him making a presentation at the afternoon South Asian history seminar in the basement of St. Antony's College in a dinner jacket. Nirad Babu willfully wants to stand out.

Whether advising a slightly embarrassed Bharatiya Janata Party leader L.K. Advani on the appropriate dress for Hindus ('Three tucks of the *dhoti*'), informing a nonplussed literary editor of a British newspaper that he does not deign to read books published after 1945 or telling an unappreciative contributor to this volume that 'I am a Hindu, and I am an Englishman', there is an impish streak in Nirad Babu that often detracts from his gravitas. As the numerous contributions in the volume make clear, he is an incorrigible tease who loves being outrageous. This forms the backdrop of the innumerable controversies that have dogged him since he dedicated the first volume of his autobiography to the memory of the British Empire in India.

It is, of course, a little more than that. In being transformed into a caricatured hate figure, Nirad Chaudhuri has been a casualty of two commodities that are pitifully lacking in India: a sense of humour and a sense of history.

Nirad Babu has a knack of driving home a point through polemical exaggeration. He has, for some time now, railed against the growing decadence of England. 'There is not a single aspect of English life to which decadence is not spreading and deepening its invasion,' he wrote in *Three Horsemen of the New Apocalypse*. However, to illustrate that decadence he chose instances that are admittedly trivial and outrageously funny.

'During my stay in England in 1955, I spoke to a lady about shops in a certain street in London. Her reply was: "Frightfully cheap!" Nowadays, when people see an article of clothing on me which they think is very stylish they ask me where I got it. When

I name my tailors, they remark, "Are they not expensive?" Shopping around has become a habit and one which repels me'.

Or take his second example, about Princess Diana.

'My wife and I were unable to share the enthusiasm which her marriage evoked. Somehow, her looks (in spite of her partial admission of her beauty) and her behaviour gave us a feeling that she was not of the class to which a Princess of Wales should belong . . . It seems to be part of a decline in the character of the Spencer family of Althorp.'

Anyone familiar with Auberon Waugh's *Way of the World* column in *The Daily Telegraph* or even with Taki's *High Life* in *The Spectator* cannot fail to recognize a similarity of approach. Enmeshed in a self-destructive political correctness that is one-tenth Islington (not even Hampstead) and nine-tenths Third World Studies departments of North American universities, the radical chic among the English-reading Indians have reacted to Nirad Babu's outrageousness with predictable indignation.

Nirad Babu's fellow Bengalis have been most angered by these affectations. Earlier this year, Professor Amartya Sen was appointed Master of Trinity College, Cambridge. It was a rare honour for a non-Englishman in this most traditional of Oxbridge colleges. Nirad Babu reacted to the news characteristically. He saw the appointment of a dark-skinned Master of Trinity as another triumph of British do-gooders and another example of England's degeneration. It is fortunate that Nirad Babu's comments did not appear in the British press or he would have stood chance of being prosecuted under some clause of the Race Relations Act. However, they were published in Calcutta and served to confirm the worst Bengali suspicion of him being as an imperialist lap dog. It is a different matter that Nirad Babu was probably just having a jolly good laugh.

Nirad Babu is temperamentally incapable of resisting either a one-liner or a put down. I witnessed an instance of a Bangladeshi scholar being left confused and somewhat distraught after an encounter with him. It was after a seminar in Oxford in 1983 where Nirad Babu read an extract from the manuscript of the second volume of his autobiography. Over tea, he held forth on Chittaranjan Das, Subhash Chandra Bose and Sarat Chandra Bose as personifications of Bengali *bhadralok* culture in the Twenties and Thirties. The gentleman from Bangladesh interrupted: 'What about Fazlul Haq?' There was a gleam in Nirad Babu's eyes as he snapped back: 'You can call him a *pathan*, you can call him a warrior, but a *bhadralok*, never.' The gentleman walked away quite devastated.

By today's standards, Nirad Babu was guilty of the most heinous violation of all the tenets of political correctness. That, however, is not the point. He was using *bhadralok* in the way it was used prior to Independence—as a status group for Bengali Hindus. Muslims were, by definition, excluded from this category, 'If anything', he wrote in *Thy Hand, Great Anarch*!, 'was self-evident in India, that was the separateness of Hindu and Muslim societies. No historical argument was too false or too foolish to be trotted out by the Hindus to contest the demand of the Indian Muslims, to have their own way of life.'

Nirad Chaudhuri has consistently decried the attempts to refashion the past in the light of contemporary political compulsions. 'The intelligentsia of my country', he lamented in *The Autobiography of an Unknown Indian*, 'have always had the faith—which certainly is justified by the secular changes in our political existence—that they are indispensable as mercenaries to everybody who rules India.' His view of history is strongly rooted in the certitudes of the past. This makes him one of the most accurate chroniclers of twentieth-century India, but it also lands him in considerable trouble.

In 1993, when the secularist intelligentsia of India worked itself into a frenzy over the possibility of India becoming a Hindu variant of Nazi Germany, Nirad Chaudhuri gave an interview to Dileep Padgaonkar, then editor of *The Times of India*. There, he contested the claim that Hindus and Muslims had always lived in peace and harmony. He saw the destruction of the Babri Masjid in Ayodhya on 6 December 1992 as the Hindu answer to centuries of Islamic vandalism. The interview—which coincided with similar remarks made by Sir V.S. Naipaul—created an absolute sensation. I came across various luminaries of Delhi who claimed that Nirad Babu had made himself available as an intellectual mercenary of the BJP. However, if they had cared to read Nirad Babu's *Hinduism*, first published in 1979 when the Ayodhya controversy was unknown to most people outside the Faizabad district of Uttar Pradesh, they would have gleaned the remarkable consistency of his views. In that book, he outlined the 'religious vandalism' of the Muslim invaders and process by which Hindus were reduced to the status of a 'cultural proletariat' and Hinduism became 'a folk culture and folk religion'. Nirad Chaudhuri was not piggybacking on a prevailing euphoria; he was merely locating an event in its larger context. Of course, it was equally bizarre to see BJP supporters claim Nirad Babu as their own. They would have found some common ground in his belief that 'While Hindu religious beliefs and practices are multiform; the Hindu religious outlook is very unitary', but they would have been deeply offended by his utter (and very Bengali) disdain for the popular culture of the *Aryavarta*.

It was a similar refusal to buckle under contemporary fashion that first catapulted him to notoriety. His controversial dedication to the British Empire in India which fashioned 'all that was good and living within us' led to his ostracism by the elite of a newly-independent India which saw itself in the vanguard of decolonization. Imbued with Jawaharlal Nehru's optimism over the future, they were unwilling to countenance the fact that the history of the British Raj in India was not an unbroken record of evil. Yet, in viewing the 190 years of British rule as a mixed blessing, Nirad Babu was not being a contrarian. He was essentially echoing the conventional wisdom of his childhood in Bengal when the peace and social stability offered by the Raj was favourably contrasted to the anarchic conditions prevailing under the later Mughals. British rule gave the Hindus of Bengal a respite and an opportunity to regain their composure.

Nor was Nirad Chaudhuri alone in viewing the Queen's proclamation of 1858 as a decisive moment in Indian history. From Bankim Chandra Chatterjee to Sir Surendra Nath Bannerjee, the benefits brought about by British rule were rarely questioned by the Hindu middle classes of Bengal. At least, not until Lord Curzon's partition of the province in 1905 shook their faith. 'British rule in India', wrote Nirad Babu in *Unknown Indian*, 'was a case of conscience with our nineteenth-century thinkers. They dealt with it courageously, with the help of casuistry in the sense accepted in ethics'.

More than anything else, it was the sustained exposure to European enlightenment that gave the Bengali *bhadralok* their exceptional status under the Raj. They may been lowly clerks in government departments or struggling lawyers in district courts, but as Nirad Babu stressed, the *bhadralok* self-image was 'in every way like the English gentry. Both regarded the general mass of the people as the lower classes, and considered themselves as the real, if not the only, Englishmen/Bengalis'. As for himself: 'Despite having lived in the city most of my life, I am a country squire by temperament'. It was this mentality coupled with their relative mastery over the English language which put them at an advantage over their 'up-country' brethren who had not entirely exorcised Mughal rule from their system.

It is important to grasp the centrality of the Raj and England in the Bengali experience. At a very pedestrian level, the Empire was all about lesser Britons lording it over the natives and perpetuating a racist regime. Nirad Chaudhuri has been unsparing in his indictment of the British Empire on this count, and he still recalls with bitterness the humiliation he felt in not being able to walk along the same path as a *sahib* in some parts of Calcutta. On a different level, however, the Raj constituted India's most organized exposure to the world economy. Calcutta was at the heart of that exposure—a possible reason why Lord Curzon who appreciated the late-Victorian philosophy of the Empire much better than his contemporaries, doggedly opposed the transfer of the capital to Delhi, an out-and-out politico-bureaucratic city. The rationale behind the importance of Calcutta and its immediate hinterland was free trade which, regardless of what nationalist historians now claim, benefited India far more than Britain. There are enough stones of the Empire around to force the realization that Bengal never had a meaningful pre-history or a worthwhile post-Raj record. The Bengali *bhadralok*, whatever his nominal origins, was a creation of the Empire. When the Union Jack was finally lowered on 15 August 1947, he too lost his way in the jungle of self-rule.

This, perhaps, was the reason why the Bengali Hindu, despite being in the vanguard of the early nationalist stirrings, faded out when Mahatma Gandhi brought the masses into politics. It was one thing to demand representative government, but the Bengali *bhadralok* could never understand why democracy had to be accompanied by an aesthetic rejection of all those symbols of British rule which they held dear. 'It was open to everybody to accept Mahatma Gandhi in his own way', wrote Nirad Chaudhuri in *Unknown Indian*, 'In the end Gandhism in politics and practice came to stand for very little else but a congealed mass of atavistic aspirations and prejudices'. It should come as no great surprise that Nirad Babu's assessment of Gandhiism was not fundamentally dissimilar to those of other Bengali intellectuals of the time, notably Rabindranath Tagore. Even those who were avowedly Congressmen in Bengal often felt the need to distance themselves from the cruder manifestations of the Gandhian order. Malcolm Muggeridge, who worked as a leader writer in *The Statesman* in Calcutta in the Thirties, detected a curious trait in his Indian friends. He wrote in the second volume of his autobiography, *Chronicles of Wasted Time*: 'Our parts in history are allotted, not chosen; and theirs belonged to the Raj which they hated, rather than to the *Swaraj*, whose coming to pass they sought.'

Arguably, Nirad Babu's demonstrative dislike of the Indian nationalist movement in its Gandhian phase was shaped by his encounters with Congressmen in the Thirties who were more passionate in manipulating the levers of power in the Calcutta Corporation than in positing a robust vision of independent India. As an editor of *Sanibarer Chithi*, a satirical Bengali weekly that revelled in lampooning Bengali notables, he got a ringside view of the seamy underside of nationalist politics. This experience plus his work as private secretary to Sarat Chandra Bose determined his judgments on the entire nationalist movement. Consequently, Nirad Chaudhuri refused to submit to the temptations of deifying a past. For all the posthumous praise that has been showered on Subhash Chandra Bose, Nirad Babu has still clung to the image of Bose that was prevalent in Calcutta before 1941: as a dogged and impetuous faction leader who was brave, patriotic but never wise. 'I think of him (Subhash Bose)', he wrote in *Thy Hand, Great Anarch*! 'as the combination of both Frankenstein and the Monster'. No wonder the Forward Bloc—demanded a ban on the book.

Nirad Babu always had the ability to distinguish between nationalism in the abstract and the Indian nationalist movement. He was among the earliest who detected what has subsequently been mythologized as the 'subaltern' current in the freedom movement. Its venality and narrow-minded fanaticism alarmed him. However, his distrust of the Anglicized upper-middle classes which controlled the Congress was equally marked. As he wrote in *Thy Hand, Great Anarch!*, 'I had found its members weak in character, mediocre in intellectual ability, and totally lacking in idealism and public spirit.' In a sense, Nirad Babu anticipated the moral fragility of the post-independence order and its inability to take India forward.

.Nirad Babu was savage in his dislike for the new class of Anglicized Indians who stepped into the shoes of the departing British in 1947. He noted how Jawaharlal Nehru loved to surround himself with Indians who had an Oxbridge education. In *Continent of Circe*, he made great play of an incident in New Delhi where he was made to change his seat at a concert on the insistence of the wife of a native *burra sahib*. He has also taken great delight in narrating the outrage of a British diplomat when he demanded the dismissal and worse of those Indian Civil Service officers who overnight switched allegiance from the Crown to the Republic. This facet of his personality may even seem inexplicable to those who see his avowed Englishness as merely a social style. The confusion is legitimate if Nirad Babu is judged in terms of the identity the Modern Indian has deemed appropriate for himself: cosmopolitan, pan-Indian, agnostic and superficially Westernized.

Unfortunately, Nirad Babu was none of these. 'When I hear my foreign friends speak of "an Indian" or "Indians" I sometimes interrupt them breezily', he wrote in *Continent of Circe*, 'Please, please do not use that word, say "Hindu" if you have in mind a human type common to the whole continent . . .' Elsewhere, in his Bengali writings, he has described himself as both a Bengali and an Englishman at the same time. At the same time, Nirad Babu revels in the fact that he is always known as Nirad Babu, not Nirad *sahib*—a subtle but crucial distinction between one type of Bengali *bhadralok* and another. The Bengali *sahib* is one who apes the West uncritically. He is the person about whom Bankim Chandra Chatterjee—no mean Anglophile himself—wrote sarcastically: 'And what shall I say of that weakest of human beings, the half-educated and brutalized Bengali *babu*, who congratulates himself on his capacity to dine off a plate of beef as if this act of gluttony constituted in itself unimpeachable evidence of a perfectly cultivated intellect?'

The true *bhadralok babu* imbibes both traditions but is, at the end of the day, a Bengali and a Hindu.

The question of Nirad Babu's self-identity is complex and easily misunderstood by those Indians who are unfamiliar with Bengali society—a reason why this volume has a disproportionate number of contributions by those who are either Bengali by birth or otherwise familiar with Bengali culture. However, the traditional Bengali, since Raja Ram Mohan Roy, has straddled the worlds of Bengaliness and Englishness with remarkable ease and without any apparent sense of conflict. He may be fastidious about his Western apparel, particularly the cut of his suits, the knot on his tie and the make of his shoes—as Nirad Babu quite certainly is. He may even know about the streets of London and the shires of England without ever having been there—as Nirad Babu did. But he would rather stay at home than attend a Bengali marriage or the Durga Puja celebrations in anything other than a *dhoti*—preferably pleated—and a *punjabi*—preferably crimpled. 'I never put off my *dhoti* for bathing until I came to Oxford in 1970, and I have to do so here because it is very difficult to dry a *dhoti*', he wrote in 1980. There is a Nirad Babu who will walk through town dressed as an English gentleman *ought* to be dressed, but the same Nirad Babu will be immaculately turned out in *dhoti* while receiving visitors at home. There is a Nirad Babu who will sneer at a Westernized Indian who does not know French, but he will be equally contemptuous of an educated Hindu who is untutored in Sanskrit. Nirad Babu is the personification of Bengali high culture—a happy marriage between the traditionalism of England and the traditionalism of Bengal. The upholder of Bengaliness sees no contradiction in a culture and lifestyle that has been the *bhadralok* ideal for at least 200 years. The conflict is in the eyes of those who are either deracinated or *avant garde.* Nirad Chaudhuri appeals to neither. He personifies the most vibrant and enlightened face of Bengali Hindu conservatism.

Which brings the subject to the equally complex subject of Nirad Babu's relationship with England, his home since 1970. Simplistic theories abound. I have met one former colleague of his in All India Radio who swears that Nirad Babu took him aside in early-1948 and whispered in his ears: 'Mark my words, in two years the British will be back!' In *Unknown Indian*, he wrote about the possibility of the 'United States and the British Commonwealth . . . re-establish(ing) and rejuvenat(ing) the foreign domination of India.' By this logic, Nirad Chaudhuri is an orphan of the Empire who just had no place in independent India. In a lengthy article in Bengali, Nirad Babu offered his own explanations which largely centred on climate and convenience. He was keen to dispel an impression that it was an inability to earn a livelihood in India through his writings that nudged him Westwards. In short, while he may well be an intellectual exile from conformism, he is not an economic refugee. When he arrived in Britain in 1970, he turned to his wife and remarked: 'I am feeling as if I was a soldier coming home from leave from a battle-front'.

'Coming home' may be another of Nirad Chaudhuri's polemical over-statements, but the expression is nevertheless an accurate expression of the *bhadralok's* enduring love affair with England that even withstood Kipling's '*banderlog*' jibes. It is a relationship that constitutes the flip side of those Englishmen who go 'native' after India. Nirad Babu is an uncompromising devotee of English institutions, including the monarchy, parliament and the Church of England. He admires the Empire and sees England as a nation that had those qualities to build the greatest empire in the world from nothing. He is fascinated by English history and England's heritage which he has systematically imbibed since childhood in Kishorganj. At the same time, he is disgusted and repelled by the England he sees around him. He is appalled by the promiscuity, by the moral laxity of the welfare state generation and the lack of commitment to the values that once made England great. To him, England does not deserve itself. 'I have now been driven back on the conclusion', he wrote in *Thy Hand, Great Anarch!*, 'because I can in no way resist it, that the greatness of the British people has passed away for ever, and the only question now is whether their last days would be serene and honourable and, hoping for the best, will be lit up by the glow of a sunset.'

Mapping decline through the grand sweep of history has been at the heart of Nirad Babu's concerns—though not, as he always hastens to add, because of his advancing years. He has witnessed Bengal's fall from grace, its effortless jettisoning of its Raj inheritance and the consequent degeneration of its culture into triviality and envy. He has been unable to reconcile himself to the self-flagellation and effete defeatism of the Hindus—a reason why he detected a glimmer of hope in the Ayodhya movement. He has been angered and frustrated by Britain's willing acquiescence in a new order that negates the very essence of its history. And he sees in the rise of America the evidence of the moral collapse of Western civilization.

There is a strong temptation to dismiss Nirad Chaudhuri as a quaint but inconsequential anachronism who harks back to an ideal age when Empire and Enlightenment blended harmoniously. It should be resisted. Nirad Babu is indeed an oddity, but his exceptional status stems from his readiness to us what we would rather not face up to. In the 100 years of being an Indian—despite all temptations to belong to other nations—he has straddled two Indias. One shaped all that was 'good and living within us'; the other provoked Pope's imagery of collapse. We may not agree entirely, but it is difficult to find another Indian who can match his grand sweep, his erudition, his accomplishments and his penchant for having the last laugh. If you disagree, just look around.

NEW DELHI
1997

SWAPAN DASGUPTA

MEJOKAKA

Krishna Bose

Nirad C. Chaudhuri is my uncle, a very dear uncle, who had a great deal of influence on my upbringing. He and my father Charu C. Choudhuri, a year older than him, were very close. In the second volume of his autobiography *Thy Hand, Great Anarch*! Uncle Nirad writes of his brother: 'We were mental twins.' When I was a small child, Father and Uncle decided that the education imparted in Calcutta schools was not worth anything. So I was taught at home by my father, just as my cousins—Uncle Nirad's sons—were taught by him. The two brothers had between them formulated a kind of unorthodox home schooling. My cousins and I are the educational products of that experiment.

In my childhood I used to call Uncle Nirad 'Bichhu', the Bengali word for scorpion. I am not very sure how or why I came upon the form of address. I had certainly no idea about the sting in his writing which would bring him fame and notoriety in almost equal measure in later years. I went on calling him 'Bichhu' until I was about eleven years old. It was only after Uncle and his family had moved to Delhi and I saw him after a long interval that the transition to 'Mejokaka' was possible.

My earliest recollection of Mejokaka is of an afternoon in our Chowringhee home. I must have been about three years old. My father had set up a separate household by that time. Before that the brothers had lived together and my mother had to take care of her husband and five brothers-in-law—all somewhat eccentric. Once Father moved out, the brothers would all get together for Sunday lunch at our place.

It was one such Sunday afternoon. Mother was busy in the kitchen downstairs. Father was in his study with the other uncles. Upstairs Bichhu and I were doing something in a very conspiratorial manner. He had a piece of coal with which he drew designs all over my face. Then he tied bits of torn pieces of cloth on my hair and my hands. I was being dressed up as a madman. Then he hid me behind Mother's beautiful, carved wardrobe. I was supposed to emerge dramatically from behind the wardrobe at the right moment. Meanwhile, Mother came up to fetch something and as she turned the wardrobe key her eyes fell on me and she screamed: 'What have you done, Khuku? Come out of that place!' I knew instinctively that adults could get away with many things and said in great panic: 'I did not do anything. Bichhu has dressed me up as a madman.' But Mother was not amused.

Father rarely took any decisions, especially about education, without consulting Mejokaka. Not that he always accepted his advice. Because if he did, I would have graduated with honours in History and not English. Mejokaka had insisted that I take up History for my honours course of studies. Decades later when my son Sugata graduated with honours in History, Mejokaka wrote:

> We were very happy to learn that you have done so well in your BA Hons. I am sure you will not think I

> am jealous of your achievement if I tell you that in 1918 I also was placed first in the first class in History at our common University . . . . In any case, after nearly sixty years a half Chaudhuri has done the same thing.

Father was one of the very few persons who could argue with Mejokaka and certainly the only one who could overrule Mejokaka's dictat with impunity. No one else in the family, not even my aunt, dared do that. I remember the occasion when my cousin Kirti was punished as a little boy by my uncle. Both my mother and my aunt were told that he was to go without lunch. My two cousins Dhruva and Kirti and I had been playing on the beach at Puri. It was during the *Puja* holidays of 1941. We played 'war'. Dhruva and I were the Allied forces and every day Kirti was made to represent the Axis powers. Even before the fight could begin, we used to tell him that he had been 'killed'. We had two airguns between us and for the lack of a third Kirti had to make do with a long piece of wood. One fine morning Kirti refused to get 'killed', chased Dhruva and with the wooden weapon struck him a good blow. That brought the punishment on him. We sat down to lunch. A variety of fish freshly caught from the sea had been cooked and served. I felt very sorry for Kirti and tears came to my eyes. Mother and Aunt were afraid and helpless. At that moment Father came in. 'What's the matter?' he asked. He was told about Kirti's misdemeanour. Father said, 'Oh, is that so? Kirti will never do that sort of thing again, I am sure. Come and sit with me and have your lunch.'

Father and Uncle were both products of the Indo-English encounter. Intellectually, they imbibed what was best of that encounter. But there was a difference. Father was not an unabashed admirer of the British Empire. So far as I am concerned, I have always been the common Indian or, shall I say, the common Bengali whom Mejokaka has described so despisingly in *Thy Hand* and elsewhere. The common person who was glad when the British faced reverses in the war. The common person who felt bitter about Britain's autocratic rule. I was unable to look upon the Raj as something which had only 'quickened all that was good in us'. I could understand Mahatma Gandhi's denunciation of the Raj as a 'poison that corrupts all it touches'.

One day, when I was about eleven years old I came back from the neighbourhood playground sobbing. One of my playmates had called me 'pro-British' because Mejokaka was broadcasting British propaganda on All India Radio. To be called 'pro-British' was the worst kind of abuse in those days. When I told Father what had happened he laughed and said I should have asked my friend what he was since his elder brother was a pilot in the Royal Air Force and was actually fighting for the British.

As a young girl I once decided to undertake a token fast because Gandhiji was fasting in prison. Father encouraged me and even observed a day's fast with me. Soon after I went to visit Mejokaka in Delhi. He teased me relentlessly about the fast. He told me how he had prepared Gandhiji's obituary to be broadcast on All India Radio. He was expected to die but disappointed everybody, so Mejokaka claimed, by not dying. Mejokaka also assailed me for lapping up what he called the 'Nehru literature' which included Nehru's autobiography of which I was a great admirer. He held very strong opinions about the nationalist leaders of this period as about everything else. To put it simply, his views ran somewhat like this: he considered Gandhiji to be a hypocrite, Nehru an opportunist and Subhash Bose a complete failure. But he used to say he at least admired Bose because he gave his life for his convictions—however mistaken these might have been.

*

At a very important juncture of Indian history I happened to be in Delhi with Mejokaka. This was during the long recess between my school-leaving examinations and the announcement of the matriculation results. I arrived at Mejokaka's Nicholson Road house on 30 July 1947 and stayed with him until the middle of September. Mejokaka has written about this period in *Thy Hand* in the chapter entitled 'Eruption of Independence'. At that time he was writing *The Autobiography of an Unknown Indian*. Every evening after dinner I lay on a charpoy on the south verandah. Mejokaka sat on the floor beside the charpoy and read out to me pages and pages of the manuscript. He was not actually reading it out to me. I was merely a symbol. He was reading it to Father who was away in Calcutta. I have vivid memories of Mejokaka reading out the beautiful passages on his ancestral village Banagram, the description of the *Puja*, the goat sacrifice, the priest who came from Matkhola to sacrifice the buffalo. The readings have left a permanent impression on me.

Sometimes he paused and even asked my opinion on a particular passage. I am amazed at my audacity when I recall how frankly I told him whatever I thought of it. I even argued with him, albeit in a very timid manner, regarding his opinions about the nationalist politics of India. We were about to become independent. While most of us were very proud to be free, Mejokaka looked upon the advent of independence as an unmitigated disaster. He predicted that in future India would have nothing to contribute to world civilization. I tried to contend weakly that though we were going through troubled times India may well emerge as a strong and creative nation. Mejokaka strongly refuted my point and said individual Indians may contribute something to world civilization but as a nation India was doomed forever. I felt very disturbed at this prognosis and sometimes could not sleep well.

My days in Delhi would begin with watching the dawn sky with Mejokaka. I woke up very early to the sound of Mejokaka's typewriter. He stopped typing when he heard me move about. We stood on the verandah and he pointed out the early morning stars to me. From astronomy he passed on to literature, then to music, to architecture, and suddenly changed to philosophy. Young as I was, this breathless exercise of intellect and erudition left me rather bewildered and exhausted.

I was sixteen when he introduced me to Plato. He told me: 'You see, when somebody comes to visit me, I open my conversation with Plato, as if he were my next door neighbour. If the visitor survives that, he becomes a good friend.' This would be followed by his inimitable, mischievous cackle.

There was always a dichotomy in my attitude towards Mejokaka. On the one hand, I was a starry-eyed admirer and proud of his accomplishments. On the other, I found myself in complete disagreement with most of his expressed views. As Independence Day approached, I felt somewhat sad and thought had I been in Calcutta I could have taken part in the general celebrations. To my surprise Mejokaka called me one morning and said I could join in the 'mafficking' if I so wished. He did not want me to feel deprived in any way. So on 15 August 1947 when our leaders kept their 'tryst with destiny'—the Union Jack was lowered and the tricolour raised—I too was one among the throng of people enveloped in dust who watched the blurry change of scene.

Then came the holocaust. Mindless violence erupted all over Delhi. 'Refugee' became a new term in our daily vocabulary. Thousands of refugees descended on the streets of Delhi from neighbouring Punjab. From the terrace of our house we watched fire and smoke rise across the city. An eighty-four hour curfew was clamped on us. Food was scarce. In a vain attempt to lead as normal a life as possible Mejokaka banned the use of the words murder, arson, loot and rape in the house. It did not help very much. But in the midst of the terrible riots I saw another side of Mejokaka. He has been always labelled 'anti-Indian'. But is he really so? In *Thy Hand* there is a description of how he breaks down after witnessing rioting and looting in Connaught Place in September 1947. He comes back home shattered. He describes how he wept and howled like a child—and his brother's daughter sat by fanning him and trying to console him with her silent sympathy. That day as I sat by fanning him I realized how deeply he cared for his country. Only someone who cared deeply could be so upset over our orgy of self-destruction.

My Delhi sojourn soon came to an end. I bade goodbye to Mejokaka who looked extremely worried as he stood on the platform of Old Delhi station which was strewn with corpses. The train moved off on a nightmarish journey.

*

Nirad C. Chaudhuri is an eloquent chronicler of his own life and the turbulent century through which he has lived. He also claims to be an historian, which he is not. What he does best are 'eye-witness' accounts of people and events. This has value when he is writing about something he has actually seen. Yet he writes about things he has not witnessed, or was not privy to, with equal confidence, refusing to rely on research, archival material or the work of others. He proudly proclaims that he has not read anything that has been written in the last fifty years. No wonder the quality of his work is so uneven—either excellent or terrible.

Of his autobiographical works, *An Unknown Indian* is a splendid piece of writing until the lengthy pontification on Indian history towards the end. *Thy Hand* has some brilliant sections, but the rest falls down, as he writes of events he neither witnessed nor researched. The only book for which he did some serious research is *Scholar Extraordinary*, his authoritative life of Max Mueller. But *Clive of India* for which he relied on his pre-conceived notions rather than any new research is an embarrassingly bad book. Some of his later Bengali work is tired, prejudiced ranting, full of inaccuracies and self-justification.

Much of his motivation as a writer can probably be traced to his childhood in Mymensingh. In many ways, he remained a child in a provincial part of British India throughout his life. His awe of the British from those days seems never to have left him. Eager to find out more about these superior imperial masters, he read as much about the English as he could and conjured up an illusory vision of Great Britain in his mind.

His description of the Calcutta of his youth in *Thy Hand* is direct and vivid. He recounts his days of unemployment and poverty in his years as a 'scholar gypsy' with disarming sincerity. Mejokaka always used to tell us never to indulge in self-pity. He tries to be free of it himself, not always with success. I have heard anecdotes from my mother of Mejokaka's life in Calcutta during the 1920s. Those were the days when novelists and poets like Bibhutibhushan Bandyopadhyay and Mohitlal Majumdar were frequent visitors. Mejokaka was going through his literary apprenticeship. Mother told me how she used to sit in the kitchen alone with the dinner getting cold. In the drawing room Mohitbabu was reciting poetry and nobody had time to think of dinner. Talking about Mejokaka's perpetual penury, Mother related to me how once they tried to teach him responsibility by asking him to take charge of the monthly housekeeping money. But having bought a couple of prints of Botticelli and Raphael he landed the household in a crisis by the middle of the month.

Mejokaka's personality was as multi-faceted as his erudition. He could be witty, mischievous, very endearing. He could also be stubborn, unreasonable and lose his temper on trivialities. Once when one of my younger uncles was getting married, all the family had gathered in our Dover Lane house for a meal. We had almost finished our dessert. Mejokaka was still on his first course since he had been giving a long lecture on various subjects. Suddenly to our dismay, he stopped eating, pushed his plate away and left in a huff. For a few minutes nobody knew what was wrong. It later transpired that the servant had started clearing the table and had picked up the first empty plate. This he had taken as a great insult. Trivialities aside, Mejokaka always remained a difficult person, unable to hold on to even his closest relationship due to sheer stubbornness and a peculiarly closed mind.

'You are very meek and timid,' Mejokaka used to tell me. 'You have to be much more assertive.' Then to my surprise he would add: 'I was like you too—meek and timid.' He told me he changed when he worked at Woodburn Park as Sarat Chandra Bose's secretary. According to him, once he came into contact with all the stalwarts of the period who visited Woodburn Park, he found most to be mere men of straw and realized his own superiority.

In all his writings Nirad C. Chaudhuri displays an irreverent attitude to the nationalist leaders and other public figures of the period. This irreverence might have been refreshing had it not been contaminated by a grudging tone. Even towards his friend Bibhutibhushan Bandyopadhyay he displays a certain lack of generosity. Even Rabindranath Tagore comes in for some patronizing treatment, although given his attitude to others he must be regarded as a great admirer of the poet. He is keen to point out some of Tagore's *atmaghati* or self-destructive tendencies and insists that Tagore must have been a deeply unhappy person.

When I read *Thy Hand* I found that he had changed somewhat his views of his great contemporaries from what he used to preach when I was young. His views on Gandhiji have remained more or less the same. He is the same old hypocrite. However, he has softened towards Jawaharlal Nehru from the days when he used to berate me as a 'Nehruite'. What baffles me is that he has considerably stiffened towards Subhash Chandra Bose who does not even get credit any more for dying for his convictions.

My marriage into the Bose family meant that Mejokaka's ill-informed utterances about Subhash Chandra Bose occasionally placed me in difficult and sometimes embarrassing situations. By now I have become used to the threatening anonymous letters, nasty pamphlets, posters in Calcutta streets and abuses in the media that follow each time Mejokaka says or writes something on this subject. 'There—that is the niece of the anti-Indian Nirad Chaudhuri' is the refrain of those who refuse to make a distinction between uncle and niece or, the other way round. He is my *khullatata*, as one Bengali daily put it preferring an archaic Bengali form for 'uncle'.

Netaji Subhash Chandra Bose in his INA phase is precisely one of those subjects about which Nirad C. Chaudhuri neither has any first-hand knowledge nor has cared to do any research. While he did see Subhash Chandra Bose at his elder brother's house in the late 1930s, he was never privy to his personal life or major political decisions. So when he confidently gives his opinions on Bose, quite apart from his prejudices he is also more often than not wrong on facts. Chaudhuri does not seem to be able to forgive Bose for not taking him into confidence about his marriage and his escape from India. In *Thy Hand* he criticizes Bose very unkindly for marrying 'a German woman who worked as his secretary'. The Austrian woman from Vienna whom Bose chose to marry was not only a devoted companion but had also made enormous sacrifices for Bose's 'cause'—Indian freedom. In writing about Bose in 1937, Chaudhuri ascribes Bose's 'rocklike opposition to British rule' to emotional instability and as explanation quotes a friend who attributes this to sexual repression. Chaudhuri is writing here of a time when Bose's relationship with Emilie Schenkl was blossoming.

Chaudhuri also tries to belittle Bose's escape from India in January 1941, suggesting that it was no escape at all because he was not under police guard. Following his release from prison after a hunger strike, Bose was not formally under arrest even though there were cases pending against him. But if Chaudhuri had cared to look through the relevant documents in the India Office Library or the National Archives, he would have found that there were at least a dozen police and intelligence agents keeping a close watch on the Elgin Road house and reporting and cross-reporting on Subhash Bose's activities, including his daily meals, in meticulous detail. Chaudhuri finds it hard to acknowledge that the imperial masters were for once caught on the wrong foot. Delhi and Bengal blamed each other bitterly for the lapse. Janvrin, the British police officer in charge of investigations, felt certain that Bose had 'absconded with some definite purpose . . . he would never I think cease to strive his utmost to achieve what has been his life's aim—the complete independence of India'. Even this British police officer had a better understanding of Subhash Chandra Bose than does Nirad C. Chaudhuri.

In *Thy Hand* Chaudhuri is very kind to my father-in-law Sarat Chandra Bose and writes with warm admiration about his magnanimity. But he misses by a wide mark the unique relationship that existed between the two Bose brothers. He insists against all the historical evidence that the two did not agree politically, going so far as to make the preposterous claim that Sarat Bose did not support and did not know of his brother's escape. The two brothers not only complemented each other's role in the independence movement, but Sarat Bose took detailed interest and even recast parts of the escape plan. Chaudhuri is angry for once with the British authorities for throwing Sarat Bose into prison in December 1941 on the charge of contacts with the Japanese. He asserts that Sarat Bose could not have had anything to do with the Japanese. The fact is that while both the Bose brothers had been critical of Japanese militarism in Asia since 1937, Sarat Bose used the Japanese diplomatic channel to stay in touch with his brother in Europe during 1941. As Sarat Bose had said in one of his speeches, if Indians hated totalitarianism they had reason to hate British imperialism more. As for Subhash Bose, he was determined to destroy the ultimate instrument of colonial control by subverting the loyalty of Indian soldiers to the British Crown, and to achieve that he had to go to territories where they had been taken as prisoners by the enemies of Britain.

About the Indian National Army Chaudhuri says '. . . the INA was made up of a body of soldiers who were most contemptible and dishonourable seen in any country or age'. Even the British had not been so ungenerous. Field-Marshal Auchinleck sensibly noted: 'It is quite wrong to adopt the attitude that because these men had taken service in a British controlled Indian Army that therefore their loyalties must be the same as those of British soldiers. I have been fortunate to have personally known many INA officers and soldiers. I have never met a body of men and women more honourable and self-sacrificing than these.' Chaudhuri is very angry with Wavell and Auchinleck for surrendering to the pressure of public opinion in India and releasing the three INA officers after the famous Red Fort trial of 1945. However, he has to concede that the Red Fort trials shook the country. 'I had passed through all the phases of the Indian nationalist agitation from 1905 onwards,' he writes, 'but never have I seen excitement and passion greater than what I saw over the punishment of the INA officers.'

I have sometimes felt baffled by Mejokaka's attitude towards Netaji, but perhaps there is no cause for puzzlement. The two are diametrically opposed in their view of British rule in India. Nirad C. Chaudhuri writes of Subhash Chandra Bose: 'He was rocklike in his opposition to British rule and unshakable in his apocalyptic belief in its end.' Well, Mejokaka was always rocklike in his support of British rule and unshakable in his apocalyptic belief in its permanence. He was in mind and temper a nineteenth-century imperialist, while Bose was a twentieth-century anti-imperialist.

Mejokaka had admired an imaginary Great Britain from afar and was bitterly disappointed on actually experiencing life in Britain since the 1970s. He then began to suffer from the illusion that the Britain of his dreams must have existed at some time in the past. He lives mentally in Jane Austen's age. Hence his eccentricities, such as dressing up in period costume, which embarrasses his close relatives and is considered bizarre by the contemporary British. He would doubtless have been happier to celebrate his hundredth birthday in the year of the Diamond Jubilee of Queen Victoria's reign than on the occasion of the fiftieth anniversary of Indian independence.

Even though I have met Mejokaka since he settled in Oxford, the last picture I would like to cherish in my mind is that of my father and uncle together during Mejokaka's final visit to Calcutta. I came into the drawing room of Father's flat and found the two brothers having an argument. Mejokaka was saying in an agitated manner, 'Dada, you do not understand anything.' Father was angrily retorting, 'Yes, you are the only person who understands everything. No one else in the world does.' I slipped out quietly. I came back after ten minutes and found the two brothers sitting side by side. Father was playing the harmonium and the two old men were singing in duet Tagore's beautiful song about the restless sojourner's quest for the distant unknown: '*Ami chanchal hey, ami sudoorero piyashi*.'

AN AUSTEN AFTERNOON

Shrabani Basu

It was an autumn day in Oxford in 1991. A low-flying helicopter was combing the City of Dreaming Spires searching for a 94-year-old writer who had been reported missing. It was after an hour and a half that Oxford police found him, exhausted and wandering aimlessly in the fields near Summertown, two miles from home. Two burly policemen winched him up, strapped him to his seat in the helicopter, and deposited him—protesting feebly—at his house at 20 Lathbury Road. The writer was Nirad C. Chaudhuri, who had walked out of his house after an argument with his wife about what wine she should serve with the smoked salmon.

This was vintage Chaudhuri the perfectionist who would never say compromise (of course, the Summertown incident left Nirad Babu feeling very very sheepish and for several days no mention was made in the Chaudhuri household of salmon, wine and helicopters).

But then everything always had to be perfect for Nirad Babu—the framing of a picture, the correct position of the music system, the right wine for the right food, the right dress for the right occasion, and the correct use of language.

'The trouble with people today is that they have lost their culture,' he always said.

It was with apprehension therefore that I made my first call to Nirad Babu. I had recently joined the Ananda Bazar office in London and I needed his opinion on a story. The year was 1988 and Britain was in the third term of a Thatcher government. I plucked up my courage and dialled the Oxford number. It was a telephone conversation I will never forget.

Nirad Babu was obviously amused to hear a new female voice calling him from the Ananda Bazar office. He decided immediately to play Henry Higgins. Within seconds he had identified me as a *purbo Bangali* (a person from pre-partition East Bengal). He next asked me to spell my name in Bengali and then in English. Then to my horror I was told that I had spelt it all wrong. If I had been nervous when I called, I was crumbling now.

The rest of the conversation (or shall I say one-way discourse) began to sound remarkably like an Ionesco play. It centred around the finer points of Bengali accents, the fine differences between those who originally came from East Bengal (now Bangladesh) and those who came from West Bengal. I was swiftly commanded to pronounce several Bengali words. I sat at my table chanting Bengali words for ten minutes. 'Unmistakeably East Bengal,' said the voice at the other end with a chuckle. A West Bengali would have pronounced them differently, he added. But I was a Bengali from Delhi, I blurted. Aha, Henry Higgins. But that too had been identified, said Nirad Babu. And the conclusion: It was plainly evident that I knew little Bengali. There was no hope for me.

I can't remember now whether I finally did get that quote I had called him about. It all seemed completely irrelevant when my Bengali had failed the Nirad Chaudhuri test.

The very next day I received a letter from Oxford. It was from Nirad Babu. He wrote he had been working on my name and phonetically it should be spelt Sravani. He looked forward to meeting me in the near future.

We spoke several times on the phone before I actually went to Oxford. In these conversations Nirad Babu quizzed me about my husband, child and family. He was horrified that I had retained my maiden name and said he would never reconcile himself to women doing these 'irrational' things. He told me in no uncertain terms that he did not approve of feminism. Nirad Babu believed in the traditional roles for men and women and nothing would convince him otherwise.

It was *en famille* that I called on Nirad Babu. Our first meeting lasted late into the night. As we walked up the path of 20 Lathbury Road, the address he has lived at for the past two decades, the little figure of Nirad Babu stood at the door ready to meet us: a small frail man less than five feet tall, in a crisply starched *dhuti-panjabi* (*dhoti-kurta*).

Years later Nirad Babu was to tell me how he enjoyed doing 'target practice' with people he met. That day I was the victim of his 'target practice'.

Having discovered that I was a student of History, Nirad Babu was immediately on the offensive. 'Who was the first Roman Emperor? Who succeeded Emperor Augustus? Who was the husband of Nefertiti?' The questions came like bullets. Needless to say I scored nil.

Question House was followed by Education Hour. By now Nirad Babu was in full flow.

'Do you know what religion is?' he asked jumping up from his favourite straight-backed chair near the fireplace. 'It is a revolt against death. A revolt against biology, a reaction against decay.'

He jumped up again (he had already left his chair about ten times in the last half an hour) to pull out some heavy gilt-edged, hardbound volumes from his vast library to point out some reference or the other. He knew exactly which page it was that he wanted. He would give me the book to hold while he quoted from memory, in Latin, Sanskrit and French. The evening went by in a whirl. Soon there was a pile of books on the floor. My two-year-old daughter lay fast asleep on the sofa. I felt I had reached saturation point, but the ninety-year-old man was weaving through the pile to fetch a few more.

Most sessions with Nirad Babu would be the same. He was a bundle of energy, a tightly coiled spring with an inexhaustible encyclopaedic mind that could handle any subject, from art to military strategy, from literature to history, from philosophy to science. It wasn't just Bengali and English literature that he had complete command of. Nirad Babu could quote endlessly in Sanskrit, French and Latin. Like a chain-smoker, he would draw from one book or subject into another.

Often he would come up with complete surprises. Suddenly in the middle of a high-intensity lecture on the rise and fall of civilizations, he would stand up and ask: 'Do you know what I think of vegetarians? They are trying to go against nature. Why are we given canine teeth? Why are we given intestinal fluids that can break down meats? If nature intended man to be vegetarian, he would have had teeth like a cow, all molars'. This was followed by a demonstration of canines and molars.

And with that he would be off again. This time to show a beautiful selection of hardbound books that he had recently bought and which he handled as delicately as china. There were certain things, he said, on which he never compromised. He would never buy paperbacks, never go out without a hat (he possesses six), never buy clothes off the peg and never count his change.

'I shall never sacrifice living to livelihood,' said the man who had once spent all his modest allowance in London buying a Saville Row suit.

It was usually in the evenings when the mood was mellow and the day's excitement over, that Nirad Babu would bring out his box of treasures. From an old suitcase would come letters from the Raj days bearing the signature of Queen Victoria. There were also old photographs, newspapers clippings, sovereigns, and more recently the CBE certificate signed by the Queen. My daughter would sit breathlessly watching as Nirad Babu brought out each object, yellow with age and rich in history and let her handle them.

When Nirad Babu was tired, he would take me upstairs to meet Mrs Chaudhuri, who by then was confined to her bedroom because of her poor health. Always dressed in a crisp cotton *sari*, Mrs Chaudhuri was the haven of sanity and organization in the house—as methodical as her husband was chaotic, as calm as he was excitable. Their tender relationship was obvious to anybody. All the playfulness in Nirad Babu would emerge when he was with his wife. He would tease her endlessly, even joking that he was going to leave her and go away with somebody young.

'She will throw you out in a day. Why don't you try and see,' Mrs Chaudhuri would reply. At which Nirad Babu would walk off laughing mischievously. Nirad Babu used to say a perfect marriage should be like a tie—either a match or a contrast. He and Mrs Chaudhuri were without a doubt the perfect match.

Apart from managing house with somebody as erratic as Nirad Babu, Amiya Chaudhuri had discovered her own talents as a writer. She had completed two volumes of her autobiography—*Didmar Jug O Jiban* (Life and Times of a Grandmother) and *Probasini Didma* (Grandmother's Memories from Outside Bengal), published in 1992 and 1994—working late into the night despite her ill health. Mrs Chaudhuri loved nothing better than to sit and chat, and the moments spent sitting in her room overlooking the garden and hearing her talk about her younger days were some of the coziest moments spent in their house.

She would giggle at the clothes modern Bengali women wore and describe the *sari*-blouses they wore in her days: with frills and embroidery and 'not an inch of exposed flesh'. She would describe how women in the olden days used embroidery to express their art. Being confined in the house most of them had no other outlet for their creativity. Mrs Chaudhuri's own embroidery was nothing short of exquisite.

Twelve years younger than Nirad Babu, Amiya Chaudhuri took care of every detail of her husband's life. Though bed-ridden herself she would make sure that his manuscripts reached his publishers in Calcutta, that the photographer was booked when he was receiving his CBE and that the meals were ready on time. If visitors were expected for tea, they could be sure Mrs Chaudhuri would have her delicious cucumber sandwiches and cake ready.

With a cordless phone by her side, she would keep in touch with the world and supervise the household affairs. She had even told her close friends that if she didn't live to see her husband's hundredth birthday, they must celebrate it with him. A morning chat with her became almost routine for me. It was Mrs Chaudhuri who would call immediately when Nirad Babu got his D. Litt from Oxford, and when he was awarded the CBE. Ironically when she died in 1994, there was no one at the Oxford house who could inform me (Nirad Babu was in a complete state of shock) and I got the news of her death via India.

Amiya Chaudhuri's death on 17 September 1994 came like a storm upon the Oxford household. Though sick and much feebler than Nirad Babu, she had been the tower of strength in the house, the anchor in his stormy life. The night before her death, they had talked till late. In the morning Nirad Babu went to fetch her a glass of Horlicks as he always did. By then she had started feeling uneasy. A massive heart attack followed and she knew it was the end. '*Ami chole jacchi*' (I'm going) she told Nirad Babu. '*Tomar ki hobe?*' (what will happen to you now?). He last thoughts were for her husband.

Her death left Nirad Babu devastated. His small frame seemed suddenly to get smaller as he cried pitifully like a child. They had been married for sixty-two years. He would describe her as 'the motor that keeps my body functioning.' It was a relationship that stood the test of time, poverty, rejection by fellow-Bengalis and sometimes abject loneliness in a foreign country. It was his wife who had managed the household through the most difficult times, encouraging Nirad Babu to go on writing. It was on her advice that he had moved from Calcutta to Delhi in 1942 and then to England in 1970. It was her firm belief that her husband's talents would be given due recognition only in England and the two settled down in Oxford.

Without Mrs Chaudhuri's support, Nirad Babu would not have made it. Few wives have made the sacrifices she had.

So completely dependent was Nirad Babu on her, that for a while it seemed that nothing could function in the house. It was

Mrs Chauduri who kept an address book and contacted everybody. It was she who kept Nirad Babu up to date with his publishers. For weeks Nirad Babu simply retreated into himself. He would spend the whole day locked up in his room, rummaging through drawers bringing out old things and crying. There was nothing one could do to console him.

Then one day, two months later, he told me that he was rearranging the house. This was always a worrying thought. It meant he would be single-handedly lugging heavy furniture around. He hated anybody helping him when he was trying to decorate and wanted to do everything himself. Nirad Babu invited us over when he had finished. The house was transformed. It was as if he was trying to capture the memories of the past several decades and freeze it in time.

The bedroom was rearranged. He said he had made it a shrine for his wife, who had spent the last years of her life confined in it. A photograph of Nirad Babu and another of Mrs Chaudhuri stood on the dressing table. He had also moved his desk into the bedroom and said he was going to do his writing in that room.

Nirad Babu seemed more in control now. He would still break down at the mention of her but he was beginning to immerse himself in his work. There were several articles that he had lined up for *Desh* and he was still working on his latest book. It was only his work, his books and his music that would help him to get through the long winter months alone in Oxford for the first time.

Before his birthday on November 23 that year, I asked him what he would like us to do. Nirad Babu came up with a whopper. He would celebrate it *a la* Jane Austen. He said he had always had a childhood fancy. He had first read Austen's *Pride and Prejudice* when he was sixteen and a particular scene had always captivated him. It was a scene where Darcy receives his lady visitors in the morning and serves them a collation. Nirad Babu had always wanted to reenact that scene. He would do it on his birthday.

On November 23 we all lined up at Lathbury road dressed in

our silks ready to act Austen's heroines. Nirad Babu was wearing his *dhuti panjabi.* The living room had been decorated in a distinctly Victorian style and in a corner stood a table with a fruit bowl tastefully decorated with apricots, nectarines, grapes and other delectables. The women were asked to sit on one side, the men on the other. We were even given little fans to fan ourselves with and look coyly at the males. Nirad Babu read the relevant passages from *Pride and Prejudice,* while we fluttered our fans delicately in the best Victorian manner. Nirad Babu had worked on the collation to the last detail. We went exactly by the book. We drank an aperitif, ate game pie (which Nirad Babu had ordered specially from a shop in Oxford), and polished it off with jam tarts and champagne. It was one of the best birthday parties we had all attended, Darcy in a *dhoti* and Elizabeth in a *sari.* What more could Jane Austen have asked for. And all because a teenager under the British Raj in faraway Kishorganj was fascinated by her story-telling.

But in all the fun and games, Nirad Babu would frequently remember Amiya Chaudhuri and feel her loss. For that special day he had worn his wedding *dhuti-panjabi.* He then took us upstairs to their bedroom where he had arranged her wedding *sari,* a *pashmina* shawl that he had bought for her and a few treasured objects on the bed. History slipped through one's fingers as one handled the fine silk, so well preserved after all these years. The *pashmina* shawl had been bought by Nirad Babu when it was well beyond his means and so had special memories. It was a pure *pashmina* shawl woven so that it could be worn on both sides.

The loneliness of Nirad Babu in that big house in Oxford was often painfully obvious. He once said he didn't want to live anymore, and that he was only living to finish his incomplete works. Sometimes he said he was frightened living in the house all by himself. Leaving him standing at the door, as we inevitably did when we said goodbye, was always a heartbreaking experience.

But the depressing moments passed as the days went on. The harsh winter turned to spring and the roses bloomed in the

Oxford house again. The child in Nirad Babu and the playfulness in him never ever went away. On his ninety-eighth birthday he played another prank on us. This time Nirad Babu was not dressed in his usual *dhoti*, but was all kitted up in a tail coat, frilly shirt with a bow tie, and white gloves. He was also very solemn as we entered noisily saying our 'Happy Birthdays'.

'Can I take your coat please, ma'am,' he said, with a completely expressionless face. Refusing to take the flowers he said, 'The lady of the house is inside.'

As we walked in bewildered, the other guests were in splits. No one explained anything. Nirad Babu did not come inside the room but stood outside with that same poker-faced expression. 'Why don't you come in,' I finally asked in desperation. 'Madam, I am only the butler,' came the reply.

Only Nirad Babu at ninety-eight could put up such an act. He continued his game well into the afternoon playing the butler to the tee. He insisted on pulling out our chairs when we sat down for lunch and wanted to serve us as well, till we all protested that he call it a day. Thankfully Nirad Babu went upstairs and was back within minutes in his *dhuti-panjabi*, transformed into the Lord of the Manor.

It was so typically Nirad Babu. Along with all the cerebral exchanges, he found plenty of time for tomfoolery. Once he insisted on making the rice himself and wanted to do it with mineral water, just to see if it tasted different from that cooked with tap water. But he told his sons not to tell their mother who would be horrified to see bottles of Evian water being used to make rice.

Nirad Babu always had a taste for the fine things in life. Even today his wine cellar is well stocked with vintages. Tell Nirad Babu about how popular Australian and South African wines were getting and he would raise his hands in horror. Wine had to be French if it had be the best.

Equally, Bengali women were among the best, said Nirad Babu. He had an artist's eye for beauty. Nirad Babu would always notice a beautiful woman or a beautiful *sari* and comment on it. Always the romantic, he would shyly recall how as a youth he had been smitten by a beautiful young woman who appeared on the balcony of a house, and the rush of poetry she had inspired. To this day he could clearly remember her face.

When Nirad Babu talked about love, relationships and marriage it was always with a certain tenderness. He and his wife had, after all, built a relationship that lasted sixty-two years.

Couples should never take one another for granted he told us once on our anniversary. Just like every garden needed watering and looking after, so also did a relationship.

Though known as the man who excluded most Bengalis from his house and who socialized with only two Bengali families in Oxford, yet the Bengali in Nirad Babu surfaced strongly on many occasions. On one of his birthdays, he said he was going to speak only in Bengali. One of his close friends, the military historian, Colonel Hugh Toye, who wished to call on him, was told by Nirad Babu that he was welcome to come but would have to listen to him talk in Bengali. Needless to say Colonel Toye spent the afternoon doing just that.

Again while he was denounced by many Bengalis as a cultural traitor and a sycophant of the British, Nirad Babu's tremendous commitment to the Bengali language would surprise his critics 'I am a Bengali and an Englishman,' he told me 'I have tried to combine the cultures: the Bengali *bhadralok* and the English gentleman, and I think I have succeeded.'

Proof that he had indeed succeeded lay in the fact that a large Bengali crowd pressed into the Nehru Centre in London a few years back to listen enthralled as Nirad Babu dressed in a bowler hat and a Saville Row suit gave a talk on Gandhi and Subhash Bose.

That his countrymen had also acknowledged his greatness was evident from the fact that Vishwabharati University honoured him this year with their highest honour, the Desikottama, and the Vice Chancellor, Professor Dilip Sinha, travelled to London to bestow it personally on Nirad Babu. At the function at the Nehru Centre on August 2, Nirad Babu received the honour wearing his *dhuti panjabi* and shawl and the D. Litt robes conferred on him by Oxford University. Round his neck was the CBE medal given by the Queen. It was as if a hundred years of the subcontinent's history stood chronicled in the shape of a little man wrapped up in silk robes and shawls, who stood straight and solemn on the stage and only said one thing, that he was not an Indian writer writing in English, but a writer writing in English. 'When I write in English I am not writing as an Indian or an Englishman. I am just a writer. Writers know no nationality,' he said.

Nirad Babu had stopped writing in Bengali in 1937. He resumed in 1966 and stopped almost immediately. In 1987 he began writing in Bengali again and was flooded with letters after his 1992 article in *Desh* where he gave a forthright account of why he had settled in Britain.

'To live in Calcutta would have been death,' said Nirad Babu whose *Autobiography of an Unknown Indian* published in 1951 provoked vitriolic attacks from Bengalis. 'I am now serving my countrymen from here. And at last, I am getting a response from them.'

Ever since he began writing in Bengali, Nirad Babu discovered that he had a completely new audience. He now receives a regular supply of letters from Bengali readers expressing their admiration for him. The letters are mainly written by young people from various corners of Bengal and till recently Chaudhuri tried to reply to as many as he could.

Once a Bengali fan wrote saying, 'If there is a writer in Bengali, it is Nirad Chaudhuri.' This gave him a 'great sense of fulfillment.'

Nirad Babu always talked about how he had never compromised in his life. 'I have never in my life applied for a job, offers came to me. The British have been very generous to me. I would not have been able to write so much if I hadn't come here. I wouldn't have lived to be my age. I was a sickly frail man.'

Frail he may have been, but Nirad Babu was definite proof of mind over matter. Even last year, at the age of ninety-nine, when his legs were giving him trouble and his eyes hurt, he was still sitting at a new word processor having figured out the forty-page instruction manual, and typing out what he said were his last essays.

He had his first article—a discussion on civilizations—published at the age of thirty in *The Statesman*. Always an arch Hindu conservative, Nirad Babu had written in another article in 1937, in *Shonibarer Chithi*, that there was no cultural bonhomie between Hindus and Muslims in Bengal. In 1966, he had also predicted an independent Bangladesh, saying that East and West Pakistan would never remain together as a nation-state. It had surprised him when Bangladesh banned the issue of *Desh* in 1992 in which Nirad Babu had described Bangladesh as the 'so-called Bangladesh.'

'They had never referred to themselves as Bengalis,' he said. 'They are Muslims first, Bengalis afterwards.'

For Nirad Babu, if there was no such thing as Bangladesh, there was no such thing as India either. He believed that India was created by the British. 'There is no central civilization and if it survives in whatever form, it does so because of the British, because of the English language. It is the ultimate irony of colonialism.'

And he does believe that India will ultimately break up 'When does religious fanaticism enter a system? When civilization and culture are not strong. Hindus have always been dominant in India. Their new fanaticism is struggling for its identity.'

No wonder then that when L.K. Advani called on Nirad Babu at Oxford in 1995, Nirad Babu was quite unimpressed. He found Advani knew little about Hinduism and his knowledge of Sanskrit was poor. In contrast Nirad Babu was pleasantly surprised by former Indian president R. Venkataraman. Venkataraman's proficiency in Sanskrit pleased Nirad Babu and he gave the former Indian president eight on ten describing him as an 'educated man.'

Another visitor to Oxford who had caused a bit of a flutter was Taslima Nasreen. The young exile from Mymensingh was to meet the grand old man from Mymensingh, and for once even Nirad Babu was quite perked up about the meeting. When Taslima arrived, he asked her English minder to wait outside since he wanted to speak alone to the lady.

Taslima Nasreen cleared the scrutiny. Nirad Babu was pleased to see that she had worn a *sari* to come and meet him, and said she had spoken to him in a cultured, decent way. Always the traditionalist, Nirad Babu had mentally drawn up an image of Taslima Nasreen as a slightly brash feminist, who smoked and defied the norms. But Taslima Nasreen had been on her best behaviour and impressed him. The two had talked about Bangladesh—actually Nirad Babu had talked and Taslima Nasreen had listened—and Nirad Babu's summing up was not too stern. 'She didn't seem to be as brash and upstart as I had been warned she would be,' he chuckled.

Always the perfectionist, Nirad Babu would say that when he wrote in Bengali he would think in Bengali and when he wrote in English he would think in English. He had no tolerance for those of our generation who spoke a mixture of Bengali and English.

He had little regard for the current wave of Indian writing in English and said that he had not read any work of fiction published after 1945. 'I will have to read ten books to find one good one. At my age I don't have time to waste,' he said.

He had little respect for the present generation British as well. England was no longer the country that he had fallen in love with after a visit in 1955—which he recorded in his book *A Passage to England*. It was now an uncultured place characterized by high taxes and cheap Japanese and Taiwanese imports. And of course, very few of the younger generation spoke 'real' English. Even the BBC's standards were falling. Nirad Babu could not live down the BBC's serialization of Jane Austen's *Pride and Prejudice* which had received such acclaim. The Beeb, he said, did not have the faintest idea of Victorian norms and etiquette and were just playing to popular culture. 'Britain is a corrupt civilization now,' he said with sadness.

His latest book, *Three Horsemen of the New Apocalypse* examines the rise and fall of civilizations. It is going to be his last book in English, since he finds it difficult to type or write now as it strains his eyes. Ironically his first article was also a discussion of civilizations.

The man who firmly believed that there could be no civilization without empires and was an open admirer of the Roman and the

British Empire, is now saddened at the complete decline of culture all around him. He clings to his lost world of chivalry, etiquette and Victorian values as the world outside nose-dives into the twenty-first century.

And as the day ends, the quintessential Bengali puts on his favourite music—*Rabindra Sangeet*—and sits back on the sofa with his eyes closed. As the dulcet voice of Kanika Bandyopadhyay fills the room his thoughts go back to his native Bengal—to a winding river, a scorching summer sun and a young teenager tripping along to school reciting Shelley and Keats, while all around him the skies echoed with cries of *Bande Mataram*. A hundred years of solitude drift by.

A SCHOLAR EXTRAORDINARY

Khushwant Singh

The following essay combines two articles that Khushwant Singh wrote on Nirad Chaudhuri, the first soon after the publication of A Passage to England *in 1959, and the second in 1988, to mark Nirad Chaudhuri's ninetieth birthday.*

'There is nothing more dreadful to an author than neglect, compared with which reproach, hatred and opposition are names of happiness.' These words of Dr. Johnson were inscribed by Nirad Chaudhuri on my copy of his book *A Passage to England.* These words hold the key to Nirad's past life and present personality. They explain the years of neglect of one who must have at all times been a most remarkable man; his attempt to attract attention by cocking a snook at people who had neglected him; and the 'reproach, hatred and opposition' that he succeeded in arousing as a result of his rudeness.

Nirad had been writing in Bengali for many years. But it was not until the publication of his first book in English, *The Autobiography of An Unknown Indian*, that he really aroused the interest of the class to which he belonged and which, because of the years of indifference to him, he had come heartily to loathe—the Anglicized upper-middle class of India. He did this with calculated contempt. He knew that the wogs were more English than Indian but were fond of proclaiming their patriotism at the expense of the British. That having lost their own traditions and not having fully imbibed those of England, they were a bastard breed with pretensions to intellectualism that seldom went beyond reading blurbs and reviews of books. He therefore decided to dedicate the work 'To the British Empire . . .' The wogs took the bait and having only read the dedication sent up a howl of protest. Many people who would not have otherwise read the autobiography, discovered to their surprise that there was nothing anti-Indian in its pages. On the contrary, it was the most beautiful picture of Eastern Bengal that anyone had ever painted. And at long last India had produced a writer who did not cash in on naive Indianisms but could write the English language as it should be written—and as few, if any, living Englishmen could write.

Nirad is not neglected any more. He has become a celebrity and the most sought-after man in the social circles of Delhi. For the last many years, he and his family consisting of his charming wife and three equally remarkable sons have been living continuously under the blaze of arc lamps. Anecdotes of their incredible fund of knowledge are favourite topics at dinner parties.

The first story I heard of the Chaudhuri family was of a cocktail party given by the late Director-General of All India Radio, Colonel Lakshmanan. Nirad had brought his wife and sons (in shorts and full boots) to the function. After the introductions, the host asked what Nirad would like to drink: he had some excellent sherry.

'What kind of sherry?' asked the chief guest. Colonel

Lakshmanan had, like most people, heard of only two kinds. 'Both kinds,' he replied. 'Do you like dry or sweet?' This wasn't good enough for Nirad so he asked one of his sons to taste it and tell him. The thirteen-year-old lad took a sip, rolled it about his tongue and after a thoughtful pause replied, 'Must be an Oloroso 1947.' I do not know if the story is true. The Chaudhuris' encyclopaedic knowledge has created a lot of anecdotes like those which grew round Professor Spooner, some true, others made up to confirm the truth.

There is little doubt the Nirad can talk on any subject under the sun. There is not a bird, tree, butterfly or insect whose name he does not know in Latin, Hindi, Sanskrit and Bengali. Long before he went to London, he not only knew where the important monuments and museums were, but also the location of many famous restaurants. I heard him contradict a lady who had lived six years in Rome about the name of a street leading off from the Coliseum—and prove his contention. I've heard him discuss stars with astronomers, recite lines from an obscure fifteenth-century French poet to a professor of French literature, advise a wine dealer on the best vintages from Burgundy. At a small function in honour of Laxness, the Icelandic winner of the Nobel Prize for literature, I heard Nirad lecture him on Icelandic literature.

This fantastic accumulation of the bric-a-brac of knowledge has been acquired over years of study aided by a phenomenal memory. His small flat in one of the old bazars of Delhi is crammed with books on all subjects in many languages. He spends a good twelve hours of the day in reading and making notes.

Nirad is a small, frail man a little over five feet tall. He leads a double life—one at home where he is his real self, a conventional Bengali intellectual dressed in *kurta* and *dhoti* (in summer only a *dhoti*), doing his work sitting cross-legged on the floor. He is a devoted husband and a fond father who has taught all his sons himself. As soon as he steps outside the house he dons a different dress and personality. He always wears a suit with a tie and carries a monstrously large khaki solar topee on his head. He is then at war with the new India of Gandhi caps and *khadi*. He expects everyone to misunderstand him and succeeds in his attempt. For the many years he walked through the bazars to Broadcasting House, the street urchins greeted him with cries of 'Johnny Walker, Johnny Walker' and chanted 'Left, right, left, right,' in time with his steps. To Indians outside his home he wants to be, and is, a *kala sahib.* That is the incarnation in which he is known to people who do not really know him; it is the Nirad Chaudhuri of the offensive dedications and not the 500 pages that follow. Nirad is quite emphatically not a *kala sahib.* He is as Bengali as his Bengali accent and he is more Indian than most Indians of his class because he knows more about his country, its history, literature, flora and fauna than almost any of his compatriots. What is more, in his own way, he has won more friends for India than those who wear their patriotism on their sleeves.

Nirad Chaudhuri is not a modest man: he has much to be immodest about. No Indian, living or dead, has written the English language as well as Nirad Chaudhuri (the only other I can think of as a peer is the neglected writer, Govind Desani.) As a matter of fact there are few English writers who have the same mastery over their mother tongue shown by this Bengali *bhadralok* in the books he has written. (Even if he were not to write another word he has an assured place in the English world of letters.) The English have been gracious enough to acknowledge his greatness. It is only in his own country that he has been denied the honour he richly deserves. The Government of India issued a fiat to its various publicity organizations not to publish anything by him; and he has been vilified by soured critics in most Indian journals. There is little doubt that the civil servant who initiated the ban never read beyond the dedication of *The Autobiography of An Unknown Indian*.

Nirad is an angry man; and he has much to be angry about. But the combination of pride and anger has made life somewhat difficult for him and his family. Success has not mellowed him.

The Autobiography, despite its greatness as a work of art, was not a bestseller. With the job gone and three growing sons on his hands, life became hard for the Chaudhuri family. Many jobs were open to him; commissions for articles and broadcasts (from foreign countries) could have come to him for the asking. But what Nirad has never done is to sell himself for money.

An incident illustrates the man's unbending adherence to his principles. Two years ago, the then Finance Minister, T.T. Krishnamachari, summoned me to his office and asked me to persuade Nirad to write a series of articles on the plight of the Bengal refugees on any terms he liked. I told the Minister of the official ban on Nirad. Armed with the assurance that it would be raised, I asked Nirad over to break the good news to him personally. When he came, I told him of the enthusiasm with which Krishnamachari (and H.M. Patel) had referred to his writing and how they were willing to give him a blank cheque and clear official objections.

He sat back in the chair for a couple of minutes without saying a word and then asked me in a slow, gentle voice, 'So the Government of India has decided to raise its ban on me?'

'Yes, it has.'

'But I haven't decided to raise my ban on the Government of India.' Without another word, he picked up his solar topee and walked out of the office.

Nirad cannot suffer criticism. He first tries to ignore it but his pugnacity soon gets the better of his resolve. *The Autobiography*, which has been acclaimed by most English critics was, due to the dedication, adversely criticized by the Indian papers. Nirad tried to take the Indian reaction in his stride. 'A hound of a good breed never pays any heed to the barking of pye-dogs,' he said somewhat disdainfully. But as soon as a leading English literary magazine came out with a mildly critical review, Nirad's dander was up. 'I will teach the . . . a lesson,' he roared shaking his fist in anger. 'Wait and see what I do to them in my next book.'

A Passage to England received the most glorious reviews in the English press. Three editions were rapidly sold out and it had the distinction of becoming the first book by an Indian author to have become a bestseller in England. The bay windows of London's famous bookshop, Foyle's, were decorated with large-sized photographs of Nirad. Some Indian critics were, as in the past, extremely hostile. Nirad's reaction followed the same pattern.

At first he tried not to be bothered by people 'who didn't know better'; then burst out with invective against the 'yapping curs.' I asked him how he reconciled these two attitudes. After a pause he replied, 'When people say nasty things about my books without really understanding what I have written, I feel like a father who sees a drunkard make an obscene pass at his daughter. I want to chastise him.' Then, with a typically Bengali gesture demonstrating the form of chastisement, 'I want to give them a shoe-beating with my *chappal*.'

*

On 23 November 1988, Nirad Chaudhuri was ninety. For over fifteen years he has lived in Oxford where he evidently intends to stay till the end—as did the man after whom he patterned his life, Max Mueller. His biography of Max Mueller is sub-titled *Scholar Extraordinary*.

Nirad C. Chaudhuri has good reasons to stay away from India. For some years he was persecuted by the government; then he received only grudging recognition for his scholarship. There were a handful of people (amongst whom I am privileged to count myself) who stood by him in his dark days and gave him the homage due to a man of genius. For a genius he certainly is. Nirad Babu has just completed the second volume of his autobiography. It should be the great literary event of 1988.

The period after the publication of *The Autobiography of An Unknown Indian* brought out the best and the worst in Nirad C. Chaudhuri. His second book, *A Passage to England*—the title being a take-off from E.M. Forster's *A Passage to India*—was largely an eminently readable travelogue though lacking in the acerbic quality of the earlier work. He had become a celebrity but being one did not increase his bank balance. He had dark moods of despair and became edgier than before. His small circle of friends which comprised the Jhabvalas, Mehra Masani and myself made it a point to celebrate Nirad's birthday by rotation in our homes. When John Freeman became Britain's High Commissioner in New Delhi, his wife Catherine took on the annual celebration in her home. An invitation to Nirad's birthday party at King George's Avenue became the hallmark of acceptance by Delhi's literary elite. None of this made much difference to Nirad's touchiness on some subjects, chiefly the chronic shortage of cash. I, who regarded it as a privilege to be able to help him out burnt my fingers doing so. I will let Nirad narrate the episode in his own words. His preface to *The Continent of Circe* entitled 'In gratitude' puts it as follows:

> My thanks are due first and foremost to my friend, Khushwant Singh, the well-known Sikh writer, good companion, and man-about-town, for the loan of his portable typewriter. Though it may be said that my mind is feudal, my hands at least are of the machine age. I can write only on a typewriter, and mine was worn out. As soon as Khushwant Singh heard that my project of writing this series of works was held up because I could not immediately replace my broken machine, he lent me his own; afterwards he presented me with a brand new portable. He is also the only fellow-Indian (significantly a Sikh, and not a Hindu) who has put in good words for me in print in India. This needed courage.
>
> But living where I live, even in feeling gratitude I cannot get away from *return indicarum natura*, one aspect of a duality in a great Zoroastrian manner, a secular conflict between Ahriman and Ahura Mazda in which light was bound to triumph over darkness. But the duality of the Hindu existence is like the cat-and-dog life of a maladjusted married couple who can neither separate nor live together. So just when, with the near-completion of one of the essays, my gratitude to Khushwant Singh was at its highest I read an account of the loan of the typewriter in public print. It was contained in a article entitled *An Interview with Khushwant Singh* by an American woman in a

magazine which described itself as 'the official publication of the American Women's Club of Delhi'—and in it I read:

> Interviewer: 'Who is the best Indian writer today?'
> Khushwant Singh: (as reported): 'In non-fiction? Without a doubt Nirad Chaudhuri . . . A bitter man, a poor man. He doesn't even own a typewriter. He borrows mine a week at a time.'

I was struck all of a heap. My poverty is, of course, well-known in New Delhi and much further afield, and therefore I was not prepared to see it bruited about by so august a body as the American Women's Club of Delhi. Why did the impressive board of twelve American women who were jointly looking after the magazine think it necessary to publish such small talk about a man who was even smaller by their standards, who had neither of the two things they understood and respected, namely money and official position? Was it because I was a writer? When I would only lament:

> *Why did I write? What sin to me unknown*
> *Dip't me in ink, my parents' or my own?*

Khushwant Singh told me that he had never made the statement in the form and spirit in which it was reproduced, and that he was not even aware of the real intention of the women he was entertaining at tea. Of course, I took his word for it. But even if in the course of a private conversation he had said all that was reported, that would not have made any difference to my affection for him. I tried to show that I bore no grudge by again borrowing the machine after the publication of the article and by most gratefully accepting the present of the new typewriter.

The conduct of the American women, however, I

> cannot even now understand unless I attribute it to the sad but inexorable law of the American impingement on Asia that the United States will never export any of its products to the East except those of which every decent American is ashamed, taken with its compliment that in retaliation, the East will set its lowest adventurers on the distributors of American money. The arrogance of the almsgiver is fitly matched by the impudence of the beggar.

The Continent of Circe won Nirad the Duff Cooper literary award. Circe, it may be recalled, was a sorceress in Greek mythology. Anyone who drank from her cup was turned into a pig. Nirad Babu's choice of titles leaves one in no doubt of the thesis he meant to expound: India is the sorceress; people who make it their home in the course of time, become dehumanized and turn into swine.

He starts off by asserting that foreigners and Anglicized Indians have never been able to understand India or Indians.

'A man who cannot endure dirt, dust, stench, noise, ugliness, disorder, heat and cold has no right to live in India,' proclaims Nirad Babu. He proceeds to describe his own habitat:

> I live just inside the old wall built originally by the Mughal Emperor Shah Jahan, overlooking a fine part and commanding a magnificent view of the famous Ridge, the Jamuna, and the Jama Masjid. It is probably the finest aspect to be seen anywhere in Delhi. My Western friends say that it reminds them of the view of the Borghese Gardens from the Pincio. But after independence, for four years, I saw people easing themselves in this park in the morning, sitting in rows. During this time the stench was so foul that after inhaling it for a year I fell ill and came very near death. Within the city I have seen streets running with sewage water and faeces floating on it while, undisturbed by this, vendors of vegetables and other

> foodstuffs were selling their produce on the adjacent pavements. I have never objected to or minded all this, and I will say that if I have any living knowledge of my country it is a reward for this unflinching realism. So, when Anglicized Indians come to argue with me, I expect them to possess at least a fragment of my knowledge and toleration of these conditions.

He quotes a story, *The Arabian Nights*, in which Prince Diamond wanted to go to the fabulous city of Wakak despite the deadly dangers that lay *en route*. Ultimately, armed with a magic weapon which would protect him from harm, he approached a sleeping giant, Simurg, who was to fly him to Wakak. To test Prince Diamond's ability to stand the ordeal, Simurg let out a stinking fart which lasted for over an hour, filling the atmosphere with a lethal stench. The Prince survived his ordeal because of his magic weapon and was able to visit Wakak. That is the kind of weapon people must arm themselves with if they want to get to terms with India and Indians.

The word Indian is a misnomer; it should be Hindu, meaning the people who live beyond the river Indus or Sindhu. Hinduism is not a religion: the concept of religion is alien to the people who subscribe to *sanatana dharma*, the eternal way. Nirad Babu divides the inhabitants into three ethnic groups; aboriginals, Mongols and those who came later—black, yellow and brown. What gave society its firm base was its caste system which remained mobile till the arrival of the Muslims. It was fossilized by the British.

British contempt for the Hindus as 'degraded, perverse, untruthful, shifty and effeminate' was far off the mark. Alberuni was closer to understanding these complex people and the contradiction in their character: renunciation and avarice, chastity with sex obsessions, morbid respect for animals with beastly cruelty, great learning with unbelievable stupidity.

'Therefore,' he went on to say, 'the scientific theories of the Hindus were in a state of utter confusion, devoid of order, and in the last resort, always mixed up with the silly notions of the crowd.' Alberuni compared their mathematics and astronomy to 'a mixture of pearls and sour dates or dung,' and observed 'that both kinds of things were equal in their eyes because they could not raise themselves to the methods of a strictly scientific deduction.'

As might have been predicted, *The Continent of Circe* did not go down well with Indians. They read it and abused Nirad in the strongest language. Nothing pleased Nirad more than being abused for the wrong reasons. He seemed to enjoy provoking people into losing their tempers. I recall one evening at the Jhabvala home when Jhab's mother was visiting them. This Parsi dowager had seen difficult days under British rule. Her husband had been a labour leader and was one of the accused in the famous Meerut conspiracy case. She was an ardent nationalist and proud of her husband's role in the freedom movement. Apropos nothing, Nirad tossed in a wounding remark: 'Parsis are not Indians; no Indian looks upon them as fellow countrymen.'

Mrs Jhabvala tried to keep her cool. But when Nirad repeated the remark, she exploded, 'How dare you insult Parsis! When you were licking the boots of the British, Parsis like my husband were in British jails.'

'That makes no difference whatsoever,' answered Nirad coolly. 'I don't care how many Parsis went to jail; Indians do not look upon them as Indians.'

Mrs Jhabvala promptly retired to her bedroom.

The trouble with Nirad was that he was always right. In my home he had a hot argument with Kingsley Martin, famous editor of *The New Statesman and Nation.* It was on some point of English history. Kingsley was a bad loser. When he found that he had lost the argument he hit below the belt. 'Forgive my drawing attention to your elegant dinner jacket, Mr Chaudhuri, but your flies are open.' The very embarrassed Nirad ran into the bathroom to button up his trousers.

At times he lost patience with my ignorance and loudly called me a fool. His wife protested that by using that kind of language he would lose the few friends he had. 'But he is a fool,' retorted Nirad, 'if he doesn't know these little things, what else can I call him!'

He could be equally unkind to his wife. She was a dark, matronly lady of ample girth. Once, when he got into the car and ordered the driver to take him home, his wife was still busy saying good-bye to her hosts. Suddenly Nirad Babu beamed: 'I must not forget the big black boiler which keeps this little engine going.'

Nirad Chaudhuri's most serious book is *Hinduism*. It is not the platitudinous repetition of what one sees in other books on the subject: Vedas, Upanishads, Puranas, etc. but an altogether novel and refreshing approach to Hinduism as it is practised and what it means to the average Hindu. He fires his first salvo in the introduction:

> Salvation is never the object of the religious observances and worship of the Hindus. The main object is worldly prosperity, and this absorption in the world has made the doctrine of rebirth in it the most appealing and strongly held belief among all the notions put forward by them about existence after death. They so loved the world that they made the possibility of leaving it for good even after many cycles of birth as remote and difficult as possible.

Just about everything Nirad has to say on Hinduism will raise the hackles of orthodox Hindus but none will be able to fault him on his facts.

Perhaps the only books that did not come up to the high mark Nirad set for himself by his earlier works are *Culture in a Vanity Bag* and *Clive of India*. The first is trivial and perhaps the product of a short phase of obsession with erotica in an otherwise sedate man. The second is a too-laboured attempt to defend a character who most Indians regard as indefensible. However, they do not reduce Nirad's stature. This very small man who, when he strode down Nicholson Road in his solar topee, was jeered by street urchins with cries of 'Johnny Walker, Johnny Walker' towers above his contemporaries as one of the intellectual giants India has produced in recent years.

THE WORLD'S LAST ENGLISHMAN

Ian Jack

Meeting Nirad Chaudhuri has always been for me a mixture of pleasure and fear, and I guess I may not be alone in my experience. The pleasure comes from Mr Chaudhuri's gifts for hospitality and fun. The fear is that Mr Chaudhuri may not, once again, find you quite up to the mark. He is a stickler for proper behaviour and a great tester of general knowledge. As this is his idea of general knowledge rather than yours, and as his general knowledge is so very general, you have a very small chance of reaching Mr Chaudhuri's mark. Then again, what would happen if you did? If you did know the names of every battleship in the British Home Fleet, circa 1916, or the names of every marshal in Napoleon's army?

Mr Chaudhuri would certainly be obliged to regard you as a more civilized human being, but he would also have lost the chance to answer his own questions. The best position in Mr Chaudhuri's company is always to be slightly more ignorant than him, so that you gain at least a little of his respect as well as all of his information.

I first went to see him at his Oxford home in the early 1980s, thanks to the encouragement of the Delhi journalist, Subhash Chakravarti, who also comes from Kishorganj in East Bengal. I had read some of his books—then more easily available in India than Britain—but, for all their bravura and sparkle, they hadn't prepared me for the dancing energy of the writer in person. His wife was still alive then a warm and gracious woman, and an excellent foil to the unflagging exuberance of her husband. Who from the outside can say what makes a marriage work? Their secrets are no business of ours, but I don't think it would be unfair or intrusive to speculate that Mrs Chaudhuri's loyalty to her husband gave him a security that he rarely found elsewhere; and that it could not often have been easy to live with a man who, in his own words, has pushed onwards and upwards through life by the brute strength of his own ego.

Since that time, as an editor, I've commissioned Mr Chaudhuri to write pieces for the Independent on Sunday *and* Granta *magazine. The letters that have come with them are a delight, written in a calligraphy which from a distance might be Bengali but which turns out to be English—as though some excited hen had walked across the paper. 'Mischief' is a word that crops up more than once. 'I might make some mischief with this piece... if it isn't suitable, I'll make some mischief with it in India.' I've always enjoyed his mischief, though his reputation for it has obscured the proper reason to celebrate him. He is one of the world's finest writers in English and his two volumes of autobiography—which isn't to discount his other work—have given the twentieth century a brave, unconventional and necessary witness.*

I wrote the following piece for the London Observer *in honour of his ninetieth birthday, in November 1987. It had one good result, or so I've been told. A year or two later Oxford University rectified its oversight and awarded him an honorary degree. I remember going to see him a few days after the ceremony. He must have seen me walking up the path, and he opened the door before I could knock. He was dressed in full academic regalia—rich red gown and mortar-board. 'Look,' he said, 'look!' He was a splendid sight. I imagine that he kept the clothes ready to receive visitors on a peg in the hallway. Who could not like a man who takes so much frank delight in himself and the world?*

Last Monday one of the most extraordinary witnesses to the twentieth century celebrated his ninetieth birthday with the publication of an equally extraordinary autobiography. Both the man and the book are, in their way, monuments to the British Empire. But while the book is big and fat—more than a thousand pages, approaching half a million words—its author is small and thin, a bird-like Indian gentleman who hops around his Oxford home, pecking at the small treasures he has hoarded during a lifetime's impecunious foraging for information, beauty and ideas.

Mr Nirad C. Chaudhuri stands five feet and half an inch in his Indian sandals and weighs six stone and ten pounds in his cotton *dhoti.* He is, as he says, 'a striking illustration of the survival of the unfittest.'

That he survives at all is remarkable: he was born a sickly baby into a home of modest means in the backwaters of Bengal in the year of Queen Victoria's Diamond Jubilee. But that he survives so vividly—any meeting with him is unforgettable for various reasons—is something of a miracle, and a tribute to what he calls his 'self-assertion through writing' which overcame the lethargy and despondency of his early manhood in India. There his mischievous indiscretions continue to make headlines ('MAHATMA GANDHI WORSE DICTATOR THAN HITLER' is the latest), despite the fact that for the past seventeen years he has chosen self-exile in England.

Here, however, he goes largely uncelebrated. Not enough people have heard of him. Nobody knows quite how to place him. He may be one of the greatest polymaths and finest writers of English prose that India has ever produced, but he fits uneasily into an age and country where the imperial legacy is divided between guilt, on the left hand, and romanticized racial nostalgia on the right.

Labour-controlled local authorities may rename streets after Nelson Mandela and libraries after C.L.R. James, but it is safe to assume that there will never be a Nirad C. Chaudhuri Drop-in Centre for Bengali adolescents in the London borough of Tower Hamlets. (He would be horrified by the honour.) None of the several television programmes aimed at non-white audiences has ever featured him, and yet V.S. Naipaul calls his first book 'the one great book to have come out of the Indo-English encounter.'

Almost all of the nine books that followed received critical attention and sometimes substantial praise. His study of Indian history and culture, *The Continent of Circe*, won the Duff Cooper Memorial Prize. His biography of the pioneering orientalist, Max Mueller, has become the standard work. His life of Robert Clive is both marvellously evocative and provocative. And yet none of them is in print. When the great wave of Raj nostalgia crashed through Britain a few years ago, Chaudhuri remained below the surface like a submerged rock. And yet he may be the last intellectual advocate of British imperialism left alive.

He has absolutely no doubts about the Empire, because he has absolutely no doubts about himself. Once he told me: 'I am what I am on account of British rule in India. And have I shown myself to be worthless? *My* kind of human being was created. Doesn't that show the nobility of the project?' The only snags were the British themselves. When Chaudhuri was a small boy, he took fright at the sight of his first white man and ran off into the trees clutching a bunch of bananas to his chest; Englishmen were rumoured to be as thieving and as treacherous as monkeys.

Little he has said or written since does much to retrieve this reputation of the British in India. From Chaudhuri's lips and from Chaudhuri's pen they emerge mainly as arrogant and stupid products of racial pride who, when the chips were down and the terrorist bombs went off, 'barked, snapped and snarled like frightened streets dogs.'

But what about them does he find hardest to forgive? *That they left*! He is still angry with the British, he says, because of their untimely destruction of 'one of the greatest and most beneficial economic and political phenomena the world has ever known.' And if you point out gently that this position contains just a whiff of paradox, then Chaudhuri will gather his *dhoti* about him and jump up. 'No, there is no paradox. In 1940 I hated Nazism, yet every day I was sustaining myself by listening to Beethoven, and Haydn. I can separate cultures from personalities, and I grieve for the Empire as an institution.'

The trouble, as Chaudhuri sees it, is that the Empire was not nearly imperial enough. The British evolved an official attitude in India which implied that, wherever possible, the native population should be left to its own devices; 'cultural proselytization' was not on the cards and Indians who absorbed Western ideas or imitated Western behaviour tended to be sneered at as the risible results of some form of psychological miscegenation. This, also, Chaudhuri cannot forgive. 'It is the meanness of their attitude. The French believed in cultural proselytization, the Spaniards believed in it, but the British behaved as though we were running away with their daughters.'

Nonetheless a synthesis of Indian and European culture did occur, particularly in Bengal, and out of it arose some of the greatest names in Indian science and letters. The most famous are probably the poet and philosopher Rabindranath Tagore, and (a consequent development) the film-maker Satyajit Ray; but any future chronicler of the era will surely have also to include this little brown man who survives still in Oxford, who fell in love with Europe fifty years before he touched it, and so enriched his life with European culture that he appears, these days, like an ardent convert in a church of unbelievers.

He has never managed to conceal his delight in learning or in himself. Step inside his house and you risk perpetual bombardment by heavy cultural artillery: salvoes of grand opera on the gramophone, followed by readings from Ronsard and Pascal, interspersed with light machine-gun fire in the shape of recitations of the best years for claret or the highlights of the Peninsular Campaign, sometimes (an odd finale) the songs of Johnny Cash. It can be a numbing as well as a stimulating experience.

Many people do not return for more, and by their absence confirm the opinion of Chaudhuri's many critics that, however brilliant, he is hopelessly flawed by bombast, showmanship and outrageous snobbery. But there is something almost touching in his lack of self-consciousness about these aspects of his character, which seem always to have existed. Consider this scene from his new autobiography. It is his wedding night in Calcutta in 1932. He and his new wife lie on the bridal bed, complete strangers to one another (the marriage has been arranged via the parents in the traditional way). And then:

> I asked her timidly after a while: 'Have you listened to any European music?' She shook her head to say 'No'. Nonetheless I took another chance and this time asked: 'Have you heard the name of a man called Beethoven?' She nodded and signified 'Yes.' I was reassured but not wholly satisfied. So I asked her yet again: 'Can you spell the name?' She said slowly: 'B,E,E,T,H,O,V,E,N.' I felt very encouraged. After that we talked about other things aimlessly and dozed off.

The new book takes its title from a verse by Pope ('Thy hand, great anarch! lest the curtain fall/And universal darkness buries all') and continues the story of Chaudhuri's life which the author began in his first book, published thirty-six years ago. Ostensibly, it deals with Chaudhuri in India between 1921 and 1952, but its true scope is much wider and deeper: Indian politics and culture, the decline of British power, the decay of the West, and (not least) the author's 'ceaseless conflict with the world in which I have had to live.' It makes many contentious judgements—when the prose comes out of its corner punching like a bantamweight—but there are also passages of great beauty.

He began work on the book in 1979 and finished the writing two years ago. There the enterprise ground to a halt. His publishers, Chatto, wanted substantial cuts. Chaudhuri refused. I first met him around that time and he was adamant: 'I don't care if it isn't published until I'm dead. I won't cut a line'.

Not for the first time, his stubbornness paid off. The impasse was resolved after some discreet lobbying by an Anglophile minister in the Indian government (which has no reason to be enthusiastic about Chaudhuri or his works) persuaded Graham C. Greene, the Chatto group's chairman, that the book should be published uncut. So when we met again earlier this autumn the author was fussing joyfully over the index and the page proofs.

He lives in a semi-detached house in North Oxford. Walking up the garden path, I could hear the soprano voice of Amelita Galli-Curci soaring from the drawing-room. Chaudhuri first heard this voice in a Calcutta music shop in 1930. It was his first taste of Western classical music and the beginning of a passion.

'Amelita Galli-Curci,' said Chaudhuri by way of introduction as we sat down. 'Do you know that I have every great singer at the Metropolitan Opera since 1902?' Had I heard of soprano X? No. Then had I heard of soprano Y, who was Turgenev's amorata? Again no.

The author made small noises of dissatisfaction, which were redoubled after he produced a Victorian book of animal stories by Andrew Lang. He had recently paid £12 for it in an English bookshop, to replace a copy he'd been given as a child. That was in 1908, when he lived in a hut with a corrugated-iron roof ('that wretched hovel') in a little town called Kishorganj. Chaudhuri was born here in the humid delta of the Ganges. The town then had a cholera season; its richer citizens were still carried above the mud in palanquins; the defeat of Russia by Japan had been heard in the town with immense elation. Asia had triumphed over Europe! The book belonged to those times.

I wondered about its author; wasn't Andrew Lang an essayist? There was a sharp intake of breath. Chaudhuri tugged at my sleeve. 'Tsk! When we mention an English man of letters we shouldn't need to explain who he was. How uneducated! Even *The Times* today writes: "Goethe, *the German poet*." What illiteracy. I am ashamed to live in England today. What a country of illiterate creatures it has become.'

But not everyone, I suggested, had his astonishing memory. In his book scenes and people of seventy and eighty years ago are recreated in wonderfully concrete detail, and all without the help of a single note (the author: 'only idiots need notes'). For five years he had simply stretched out on his floor—his usual writing posture—and filled page after page with his fountain pen. Surely this was remarkable for a man approaching ninety?

'No, no, no. I reject that. Memory is a product of interest in life. The price of potatoes I can never remember, but dates I have given all from my memory and have found them to be correct. I don't memorize. It comes. I'm interested.'

I mentioned one particularly striking passage in his book, which deals with his realization that the landscape of Bengal could contain beauty. Previously he had imagined, through his schoolbooks, that Wordsworth's England held the monopoly.

> It was on 14 April 1913, that I was going from Goalundo Ghat to Narayanganj in the river steamer *Condor* . . . The Padma, though very wide in this region, is a comparatively shallow river with many sandbanks. It being early summer, these had already risen above the water and made the river a mass of serpentine streams, like the background of Mona Lisa, of course with this difference that there were no rocks . . . The light on the river was like moonlight but on the sandbanks it was that of sunset. How that happened I cannot tell.

Later the steamer swings round 'twenty-four degrees to port' and goes ahead 'past the great pagoda of Rajabari, with the engine thudding and the paddles clunking.' Chaudhuri has not been near these scenes since the 1920s. Again, couldn't this be described only as an astonishing feat of memory—the ship's name, the precise date, the degree to port?

Chaudhuri shrieked—'hee, hee'—and said he had been looking into the binnacle at the time. Also: 'I was taught that before I went on to a ship to know its name. Shall I give you the British battleships of 1939? I give you . . .' He began a chant like a temple priest. '*Royal Sovereign, Royal Oak, Ramilles, Resolution, Revenge, Queen Elizabeth, Warspite, Barham, Malaya, Renown, Repulse, Hood, Nelson, Rodney*.'

It was one his naval days.

'I can give you the Japanese battleships too . . .' (and he began to). He indicated his prints of Napoleon. 'Why have I got them? Because as children we were great admirers of Napoleon. Before I was sixteen I knew the entire Italian campaign by heart. Now I shall tell you the names of all the twenty-two marshals of Napoleon' (and he did so).

Later he recited extracts from Ronsard, Tagore and the Ramayana in their appropriate languages, enumerated the piano sonatas of Beethoven, then his quartets, then the number composed in the minor key. It was as though some celestial cigarette-card collection had been emptied over our heads. How could he retain so much information on so many disparate things?

The author clucked. 'Because I'm a man. We in India before 1920 were entirely trained on the renaissance model of the *uomo universale*, that is to say if a man is to be whole he must be interested in many things. Listen, I came to Europe for the first time in 1955 at the age of fifty-seven. And do you know that I could walk between Kensington and St. Paul's without once asking for directions?' The morning progressed and layers of the author's life accumulated on the floor. Precious books bound in calf on which Chaudhuri had once expended three months' salary; photographs ('my friend Lady Diana Cooper'); gramophone records. Chaudhuri danced through them to pluck down more books from the shelves and issue injunctions: 'Look . . . listen . . . see!' He has, as he says, retained to old age a sense of wonder which is like a child's. Lunch arrived. The wine was good and the food delicious, a mixture of English and Bengali dishes cooked by Mrs Chaudhuri, who fifty-five years ago in Calcutta spelled out Beethoven on the marriage bed. 'One thing she knows about me,' said the author. 'Whatever I may boast and brag about, at bottom I am not a bad fellow.' His wife fiddled with her *sari* and smiled. And I was chided only twice; for describing the cognac as brandy and for holding my hock glass by the bowl rather than the stem.

Sometimes, said Chaudhuri, he imagined he had been put on this earth simply to demonstrate to Britons how their grandfathers wrote, how they behaved, and how they drank. He has Quixotic notions of a departed chivalrous age. As he says in his book: 'It is a fatality with me that wherever I go, the spectre of decadence treads at my heels like the Foul Fiend.'

All this, the talk, the books and the wine, might lead to the impression that Chaudhuri is well off, with an academic sinecure and a place at some High Table. Not so. The Chaudhuris live in a rented house and depend for their comfort on special security, small royalties and the kindness of relatives and friends. He has no connection with Oxford University and many stories relate to his difficulty as a college guest. His only degree, apart from an honorary doctorate from Stirling, is a first-class BA from the University of Calcutta. Almost all his prodigious learning, even his French and German, comes from self-tuition.

He is full of maxims and cheerful nonsenses. Never drink a champagne less than Dom Perignon. Good English can never be written on a diet of Indian food. Indians look bad-tempered in this country because they have adapted too readily to the lavatory seat ('They will never get clean bowels until their knees touch their armpits. I, on the contrary still perch like a fowl. Hee, hee').

Listening to these Johnsonian strictures, it is easy to forget how late life has blossomed for him. He saw the sea for the first time when he was twenty-seven and the hills at close quarters when he was thirty-four (and got so excited by the gradients and the views that he made himself ill through exhaustion). He was forty-five before he put on European clothes. He did not taste wine until he was fifty. His first books appeared when he was fifty-four. And he was nearing the end of an average Indian male's lifespan when he found his way so effortlessly between Kensington and St. Paul's.

He likes to compare his ancestry to the minor French nobility, but in fact his immediate background is Hindu middle class. His father was a minor lawyer in the small town of corrugated-iron roofs, and Chaudhuri first went to work (reluctantly) as a clerk in the Department of Military Accounts in Calcutta. He freelanced as a journalist for a time but never became a professional reporter ('I had too great an intellectual contempt for those I would have had to interview').

Often he was unemployed. His salvation came from an unlikely quarter given his present imperial views. He became secretary to Sarat Bose, elder brother of the leader of the Indian National Army, and then at the beginning of the war moved to Delhi to take a staff job with All India Radio. Poverty, until that moment in his middle age, was never far from the door.

Books were the problem. His whole life symbolizes the power of the written word to lift horizons and widen attitudes; a power since ceded to moving pictures. He cannot remember the time, he says, when he did not know the names of Queen Victoria, Prince Albert, Napoleon, and Raphael.

His life as a clerk ('drab and mean') was enhanced by subscription to the *Times Literary Supplement* and the *Nation* and *Athenaeum*. Margot Asquith's autobiography showed that life could be a romp. He began a correspondence with Arnold Toynbee. And in the meantime he spent recklessly. He ordered books from Paris and London—twelve volumes of Pascal bound in calf, a special edition of Casanova on Chinese bamboo paper—while for his three sons he bought Lott's building bricks and clothes from the best English shops. The debts piled up and sometimes the moneylender's men besieged the house.

The shame and hardship are evoked vividly in his autobiography but he does not expect pity and neither does he give it. He thinks compassion is a weak-minded vice which corrupted and eventually ruined an empire's power to do good. He can talk as fearsomely and smugly as any hard-faced man who did well out of a war.

Over the coffee he said: 'You have seen the horrible poverty in India, and yet has it damaged me? That poverty degrades anybody is a fallacy. You (in the West) are being cheated by all those countries which will not help themselves. In India all my life experience has been: no efficiency is rewarded, no inefficiency is punished. The fundamental attitude is that it is the duty of the rich to help the poor, and the poor shall do nothing. That is the system you are helping. That wretched popular singer Geldof! I would have hung him.'

In 1951 Macmillan published his first book, *The Autobiography of an Unknown Indian*, in which Chaudhuri described his early life with considerable pungency and skill. Chaudhuri had always worshipped European civilization, now European civilization acknowledged its distant devotee. The London critics sat up and took notice. *Autobiography* was reviewed by Harold Nicholson in *The Observer* and Raymond Mortimer in the *Sunday Times.* Tagore apart, no other Indian author had excited such attention in the West. But the reaction in India was not so favourable. Chaudhuri had dedicated his book to 'the memory of the British Empire in India . . . because all that was good and living within us was made, shaped and quickened by the same British rule.' Independent India was then only four years old.

Increasingly Chaudhuri found himself isolated (sometimes mocked) by the role he had created for himself—a self-confessed 'controversialist' who despised the new India and zealously pursued European tastes (wine, porcelain, tweed jackets) which he could hardly afford. He lived then in a modest flat near the walls of old Delhi—the cheaper quarter of town—decorated with a reproduction of the Rokeby Venus whose nudity (he is pleased to say) scandalized visiting Hindu gentlefolk.

Today in England he is equally isolated. Perhaps he would be unhappy if he were not; he has always possessed, as he himself writes, 'a perverse ability to make the worst of both worlds.' Few of his fellow-countrymen call on him ('Indians do not come here, they feel uncomfortable') but Chaudhuri says he does not miss their company or much about India itself. His civilization, Victorian and Edwardian Bengal, is dead; killed by Partition (his birthplace is now in Bangladesh) and political and social turmoil.

The great rivers of his childhood are now just a lining to his heart. He has not seen them since 1927. 'Never return to the East' is another of his maxims. He has always moved West: from East Bengal to Calcutta, from Calcutta to Delhi, from Delhi to Oxford. He insists he will never go back.

His ego's route to the next world must lie in the promising but treacherous eye of the setting sun.

TO NIRAD C., WITH LOVE

Amita Malik

The first glimpse I had of Nirad Chaudhuri was just before Independence. I had come to Delhi for an interview to get into All India Radio. The train from Lucknow arrived very early in the morning and I was trying to get to New Delhi from the Old Delhi railway station in a *tonga*, a shaky carriage drawn by a half-starved little pony. On the wide stretch of road, just before Kashmiri Gate, I noticed a diminutive man, in a suit and tie with a hat on his head, walking at a steady, very fast pace. You could not have missed him, because he looked so incongruous in the middle of obese Indians in various stages of Indian undress, also taking their much slower constitutionals.

I was duly interviewed for All India Radio and joined within a month. Like all novices, I was put on early morning duty and on my very first day I found the same diminutive man, again in a suit and tie, trotting briskly along the corridors of Broadcasting House and vanishing into the News Room. Soon enough, I found out it was none other than Nirad C. Chaudhuri, Talks Officer in the Counter Propaganda Unit of All India Radio. His much younger colleagues were all in awe of him, not only because his English was formidable but because he had worked as secretary to the politician Sarat Chandra Bose, the elder brother of Subhash Chandra Bose, then very active with the Indian National Army and giving the British many anxious moments. Add to all this the fact that Nirad C. seemed to be an expert in war strategy and their devotion was complete. For instance, he was able to forecast to the day when the Japanese would use elephants in Burma. Now while this might have staggered his colleagues, the British, it seems, suspected him of being a spy, although no one seemed to know for which side he was spying or why he should let out all the tactical secrets of the Japanese if he was indeed on their side.

Then one day, I found that there was an exhibition of Gauguin prints in the temporary art gallery next to Broadcasting House in some hutments put up by the Americans during the war. As I entered the art gallery, I found Mr Chaudhuri, followed by three little boys who were pocket editions of their father, being conducted round the exhibition with a fascinating commentary by Mr C. I followed as closely as I could and I should say it was the best lecture on Gauguin's masterpieces that I would ever be privileged to hear. Soon I was introduced to Mr Chaudhuri by some of his younger colleagues who were good friends of mine but, although he always kept his stiff demeanour, he was always polite and kind if I ever asked him questions about broadcasting or the performing arts. In fact, he was an encyclopaedia on every subject under the sun and I took full advantage of it when I was too rushed or too lazy to look up reference books.

One day on the sunny verandah outside the Western Music Section of All India Radio, of which I was in charge, I found I was fast losing an argument about Atonal Music which I had rashly started with Professor Jackson of the Royal Academy of Music whose piano recital I had just recorded. To my vast relief I found

Mr Chaudhuri walking past us at his usual brisk trot, looking straight ahead. I immediately stopped him and handed over the argument to him. A stunned Professor Jackson, who had so easily scored against me, found himself floundering before the aggressive erudition of Nirad C. I shall never forget the look of amazement on his face as Nirad C. floored him with ease. And I have since learnt to my cost, as have several others, that you can never, but never, win an argument with Nirad C. because he is an expert on every subject possible. And the sooner one realizes this, the better.

Soon after, Nirad C. left All India Radio, following his persecution by the Government of India for giving his famous first book, *The Autobiography of An Unknown Indian* to Macmillan's (he wrote directly to Harold Macmillan about it). He had sent it for publication without getting departmental permission. He was at a very loose end after leaving AIR and put to inevitable financial hardship until the French ambassador to India, Count Ostrorog, tactfully gave him an assignment with the French Embassy in Delhi. At one of the official French receptions, I made the acquaintance of Mrs Nirad C. and I found she was the very opposite of her husband as far as personal relations were concerned. She hugged me warmly and reminded me that she had known my mother very closely in Shillong, where I had grown up. She said I was a very naughty child and that once when my long-suffering mother had almost caught me to give me a well-deserved whacking, Mrs C. had admired my agility in diving under the long dining table, where my mother could not follow me, and then escaping into the back yard of the house where I hid until it was safe to come back.

Soon enough I discovered that Amiya Mashi (Aunt) as I called her, was in no way in awe of her husband. This was proved when their son Dhruva, the famous photographer, who has taken some of the best photographs of his father and mother, held his first exhibition in New Delhi. I was now a journalist and walked over from *The Statesman* office, which was opposite the building where a room had been taken over for the exhibition. I arrived early to help out. And I found that Nirad C. had transported a highly valuable Spode tea set from his house to serve tea to the journalists and photographers invited, who were not exactly used to such delicate china. Sure enough, one over-enthusiastic cameraman knocked over a cup and saucer for all the world to hear and the whole team of journalists and photographers soon left in embarrassed silence. 'I told you so, I told you so', said Amiya Mashi sternly to her now sheepish husband, 'I told you someone would break something and spoil the set.' 'It's all right, I'll ask Harrods to send me a spare', said Nirad C. bravely. 'You know as well as I do that you can't get a replacement,' said Amiya Mashi with a note of finality in her voice. For once, Nirad C. had no answer.

At the next reception at the French ambassador's I heard Nirad C. complain that he was finding it difficult to get celery for some exotic French dish his wife was cooking for some guests. I said I had some celery growing in my garden, not prime quality but good enough for flavouring and said I would be happy to give him some. I was promptly invited to his house in Kashmiri Gate to deliver it. There was no difficulty whatsoever in locating the building, because Nirad C. was now a celebrity and his humblest neighbours were ready to give directions. Besides, there was Nirad C. peeping from the balcony, clad in the traditional Bengali indoor wear of vest and *lungi* and waving me up the stairs. Knowing how fussy he was about punctuality, I had arrived exactly at 11 a.m. and was promptly offered some cognac. 'What, at 11 o'clock in the morning', I rashly exclaimed. 'Is there any reason you should not have cognac at 11 o'clock in the morning?' countered Nirad C. 'I suppose not', I murmured feebly and then thoroughly enjoyed the cognac which was of the very best and served in an exquisite cognac glass. Soon Nirad C. pulled down some bottles of wine from a shelf and gave me a long lecture on their district, their vintage and their special qualities. Neither he nor his sons drank wine, but he was of course an authority on wines too and his sons, not yet in their teens, could take one brief sniff from an open bottle and locate the wine and the vintage.

Years later, when I drove down from London to spend the

day with Nirad C. and Amiya Mashi at Oxford, I was told by Nirad C. immediately on arrival that I would get a Bengali lunch and a European dinner. I have no idea how Amiya Mashi managed to get hold of the ingredients, but the Bengali lunch was a classic, beginning with *shukto* (mixed vegetables with a slightly bitter flavouring) and ending with *tok* (a sweet and sour fresh chutney). We ate it in peace because even Nirad C. refrained from lecturing me on Bengali food which I had eaten since childhood and cook quite well, although not as well as Amiya Mashi. But when it came to the European dinner, it became one long harangue. From sherry to cognac and all the wines in between, he analyzed them in detail and told me how one particular white wine from Germany (which I think went with the fish) was made from grapes which had to have frost on them to give the right flavour. He asked me if I would like the cheese before the dessert, as in France, or after, like the British. After a time I did what Amiya Mashi usually did. Listened to him and then did exactly what I liked.

I wonder how many people know that Amiya Mashi brought out in the early nineties an excellent paperback called *Traditional Indian Cooking*, with some easy-to-follow Bengali recipes. It has a masterly essay on Gastronomy in India by Nirad C. Chaudhuri. An unconcerned publisher did not project it properly and very few people got to know about it. It certainly needs reviving in the hundredth year of Nirad C.'s life.

At another French reception, I had discussed with some guests how Nirad C. had written that because they were the fairest in complexion, Punjabi women were the most beautiful in India. I considered it betrayed not only colour prejudice but was also an insult to other Indian women and particularly Bengali women. I wrote and said so in an article in the *Illustrated Weekly of India*. Next day I got a hand-written note from Nirad C. on the French ambassador's personal stationery. 'Dear Amita,' he began, 'It was very snide of you not to mention the subject to me when we met at the French ambassador's last evening...' However, I soon I had my revenge, or perhaps I should say he made retribution, because some years later he wrote a book in Bengali called simply *Bengali Women.* He sent one of the first copies to me, which he endearingly inscribed: 'To Amita, ONE of My Bengali Sweethearts.' I sent him a thank you note, but added: 'What do you mean ONE of your Bengali sweethearts?' I had forgiven all, because in the book he now put Bengali women at the top of his ranking list. Because, he said, he had applied to them his most acid test. On a visit to Calcutta after over twenty years, he had kissed the hand of every Bengali woman he met, from a child of two to an eighty-year-old woman. And they had all accepted the gesture with poise and sophistication. *Voila.* Top of the list.

Some years later, I persuaded All India Radio, which he had left in anger many years before, to let me interview him. It was a characteristically fiery interview, which, incidentally was never broadcast, because AIR was too scared. If they have kept the tape, which is unlikely, because AIR has no sense of archive value, I feel they should have retrieved and broadcast it in Nirad C's centenary year. When he arrived at Broadcasting House for the recording, he was received with great warmth by the AIR staff, including the Director-General and his old colleagues in the newsroom. When he left the studios after the recording, he was also escorted out with great ceremony. Before leaving, he meticulously shook hands with everyone present and then it was my turn. I pointedly pushed forward my hand, but pointing upwards, and said: 'Aren't you going to kiss my hand?' It is the one and only time I have found Nirad C. acutely embarrassed. He just fled into the car without a backward look. And I think one reason he has always been so fond of me is because right from the start I have treated him with respect, but also cheeked him whenever I got a chance. Since hardly anyone else dares, I think he has enjoyed my cheek as much as I have because it has proved he is human. And I think beneath that forbidding exterior, a very warm human being.

The last time I visited him in Oxford, Amiya Mashi was still around, but gravely crippled with arthritis. When I entered the house, Nirad C. was listening, I think to Monteverdi. He asked me how I had come and I said in Bengali: 'Bus *ey elam.*' (I came by bus). He immediately picked on the word *elam*, which he said was East Bengali and asked if any of my ancestors were from what is now Bangladesh. I admitted some were. So he immediately went off into a learned discourse on the Greek language and told me how there were parallels in Greece to people from different regions using different words for the same thing. To make a very poor pun, it was all Greek to me. And after he had finished, he waved towards the kitchen and said: 'Your Mashi is there.' It was a sad sight to see Amiya Mashi, her fingers cruelly crippled with arthritis, cooking a Bengali *khichuri* (rice with lentils) for me and, leaning painfully against a tea trolley deep-frying some *phuluris* (vegetables in batter) to go with the *khichuri*. I hastily offered to help, but she roundly scolded me: 'Do you think I am so decrepit that I can't cook for you any more?' And so she did and laid the table and served the dishes before eating. And that was the last time she cooked for me....She did not tell me that it had taken her twenty minutes to come down one flight of stairs from her upstairs bedroom to the kitchen. But she did show me proudly the manuscript, which she was writing equally painfully, of the second volume of her memoirs in Bengali. The first had been a tremendous success.

I think Nirad Chaudhuri would not have been what he is without the patience and unfailing support of his wife. She cooked him exquisite food, including the most difficult Western food to satisfy his fussy appetite and looked after him with care and devotion, pulling him up when necessary, which is possibly why he has lived to be a hundred. And although I can imagine him without her, I could never have imagined her without him. They were a perfect couple. I am not surprised he did not go to her funeral. It might have killed him. And now his loneliness must be complete, but he will never show it. Because now writing is his whole life and write he will, till the very end, full of fire as ever.

I have always found it intriguing that Nirad Chaudhuri has faced more flak from his fellow Bengalis than anyone else. This is understandable during what they consider his pro-British phase. My otherwise calm and cool brother-in-law started frothing at the mouth, and perhaps one cannot blame him, when Nirad C. said somewhere that British cats were superior to Indian. That was long ago, when Chaudhuri was still raving about the British and had decided to settle down in England. And now he is one of the severest critics of the decadence in British life and its fallen values. But even when India was celebrating its fifty years of independence and when Nirad C. was about to complete his century, there were angry letters in the press protesting about Tagore's university Shantiniketan conferring its highest honour on him. A writer quoted Chaudhuri at length about something critical he wrote years ago about Tagore and Shantiniketan. And said that Shantiniketan has let down the team.

I find all this very petty, because Nirad Chaudhuri, long before Rushdie, Vikram Seth, Arundhati Roy and the rest, took the international literary world by storm, completely single-handed and without godfathers, with his *Autobiography of An Unknown Indian.* Not least of all because of its masterly use of the English language. It still remains perhaps the best picture of growing up in India ever written. And will remain a classic of its kind well beyond the twentieth century.

THE LITTLE BIG MAN

Nabaneeta Dev Sen

When I met Nirad Chandra Chaudhuri for the first time, at 41 Harefield in the early Seventies, the sprightly little man with quick, birdlike movements reminded me of a sparrow. Not in the Chaucerian sense—no, he does not bring lechery to the mind—although he does indulge in a lot of risqué talk for which he unfailingly begs my pardon. But his risqué talk is highly Victorian and quite funny because they are not meant to be jokes but serious social comments. Visually I found him very attractive, a diminutive man, always impeccably dressed as a Bengali *babu* in a Bengali silk *kurta* with gold buttons and an expensive *dhoti*, weightlessly bouncing up and down the stairs, in and out of chairs, prancing around the room bringing books out of the shelves, fetching rare bottles of wines (purely as exhibits) from the cellar, spreading out maps on the table, putting records on the gramophone, and chatting incessantly while going through all these activities. He is tiny and delicately built, with a large head, out of proportion with the rest of his body, and bald, therefore closely resembling a cartoon. And his springing movements also remind one of animated pictures. (He especially reminded me of an old comic character I knew as a child, who has since disappeared, called Mr Magoo.) Watching Nirad Babu seemed in itself an engaging act, he is not boring for a moment even if you are not listening to his words. But then if you do, you would be even more engaged, may even be enraged, since that is always his aim, and very often he succeeds. He intends to try his guests' patience teasing them, and testing them, as if he gets a malicious delight out of annoying people, pushing them to the end of their tether.

Nirad Babu comes through as a bright, shining, razor-sharp, deeply embittered, lonely, restless man, who believes he knows more of everything than anyone paying him a visit might. Generosity is not noticed in his words but self-aggrandizement is, politeness and humility are not his cup of tea, but aggressiveness and arrogance are. The funny thing, however, is, that like the way he dresses both at home and outside (in a three-piece suit, frilly shirt, bow-tie, bowler hat) he genuinely wants to believe himself to be an old-fashioned gentleman, and he claims as much. But he has his own idea of gentlemanliness which may not match those of others. About fifteen years ago, one afternoon I was planning to visit him along with a friend. I called to make sure it was okay. He wanted to know the name of my friend, and when he heard it he told me his mind in no uncertain terms. 'You are most welcome,' he said, 'but not your friend. I don't want her in my house.' I was shocked and excused myself saying that I would drop in some other day when I was alone. It turned out that he had had an altercation with this lady in the pages of a Bengali weekly some ten years before that, and had not forgotten nor forgiven her since then. This had surprised me, since the person concerned was younger than his sons, and such ungenerous behaviour was not expected of a man approaching eighty. But later, on thinking it over, it appeared to be a singular act of honesty, one I myself am not capable of performing. We are all ensnared by hypocritical practises known as 'social grace'. Nirad Babu does not care for it. Although, he can be very warm and gracious when he so wishes, and I have seen many instances of that in the last twenty-five years.

In conversation, Nirad Babu is exceedingly impressive and he works hard at it. Just like he does in his writing. In both cases he performs alone. In his writing he can be charming as he can be maddening, and always bristling with information and opinions. Not only does he enlighten and entertain in the best of neoclassical tradition, he also enrages his readers every so often. In his Bengali writing, his wit is sharp, his analysis brilliant, his point of view original—yet, the taste it leaves in the mouth is mostly bitter-sour. Sweetness is hidden in the private person and reserved for a few, the public persona carefully avoids it. He is hot and acrid for the benefit of the world, and that is how he was when I met him twenty-five years ago.

I had known two of his brothers earlier, an older and a younger one, both friends of my father. Although the brothers have a striking physical resemblance, they did not share their personalities. Charu Chandra Choudhuri was much older than my father, and I have known him as a quiet, affectionate person. Dr Khirode Choudhuri was bursting with energy, like Nirad Babu, he was a small but sturdy man with a hearty laugh and a lot of fun. He happened to be my doctor when I was a child (also my daughter's) and was kind to me and to my pet animals. Nirad Babu looks much like Khirode, and shares his excessive energy, but that is probably where the resemblance ends. He loves fun, but always at the expense of others, and I wonder whether he can have patience for pets and children, creatures who cannot share his adult world of books and paintings, classical music and vintage wines.

Nirad Babu is not a social creature. Although he needs company to disseminate his thoughts, he is not interested in other people's thoughts. Today he has no patience to listen to others. He asks no questions, except when he knows the answer and expects his guest not to know it. He does not believe that anyone else may have anything of any importance to say after he has spoken. Everything that was worth knowing has already been written down by historians, scientists, poets and philosophers and Nirad Babu has had the time to read them all. What remains is the scum and need not be read.

I had once taken a picture of Nirad Babu in Harefield, sitting in front of the photograph of a Royal Bengal tiger. Their spirits matched perfectly. The same time I had taken another picture of him in his garden, tending a rose, kneeling on the wet soil. A picture of delicate care and nurture. That is also very typical of Nirad Babu. He has a green thumb, and grows fabulous roses, which he proudly shows off. With equal pride he shows off his son, historian Kirti Chaudhuri, whom he had not sent to any school, but tutored at home, all by himself. And who did brilliantly at college, in the best of British universities.

'I wanted to be a historian and write a comprehensive history of culture,' he told us in June (1997), 'but when I was fifty and saw this was not going to happen, I thought of writing an autobiography, and started on it—in 1947. Once it was finished, I looked for an agent in England, for English books should be published in England and read by the English-speaking people. In 1951 the book came out and my life changed from that day.' He was saying this to my daughter whom I had taken with me to visit the legendary figure of this century. It is not every day that one meets a centenarian, let alone a Nirad Chandra Chaudhuri. But my daughter did not jump to grab this rare opportunity, her friends had discouraged her. 'You'll have to wear a *sari* if you go to see him,' they had warned her. She was in jeans. I bargained, we settled on a roomy shirt instead of the skimpy summer tank top over the jeans and we went. 'Don't tell him you are acting in a film, a Hindi film at that, he hates pop culture,' her well-wishers warned. 'In any case you are a student, just tell him that.' They were worrying for nothing. We didn't have to tell him anything. Nothing at all. Not even her name. He was not interested. I tried to introduce her. 'My daughter...' I began. 'I know! I know!' came his response, as I bent to touch his feet. When she touched his feet, he remarked, 'The gesture doesn't go with your dress.

Pranam does not become one wearing pants.' A piercing look came from her in my direction. She said nothing. I did: 'What do the men wear when they touch your feet, Meshomoshai?' Fortunately for him he has partially lost his hearing, at least for such insignificant private conversations, so he ignored my question and declared: 'I shall be a hundred years old if I live till the twenty-third of November, this year.'

'Of course you will!' said I offering the small gift I had brought for him. He thanked me gracefully and began to talk. In the middle of the speech he stopped and requested his son Dhruva to make some tea for us. We didn't want any tea, and said so. 'But how can I believe you?' he asked, 'Bengalis say "no, no!" then go home and tell others "he didn't even offer us a cup of tea"!' Well now we wouldn't be able to do that.

In 1994, when I visited him in Lathbury Road, Mrs Chaudhuri was not keeping too well, she was confined to her bedroom upstairs. Nirad Babu had taken me up to her room and offered me tea or coffee. 'Who will make it? You, or me?' 'Me, of course,' came the chivalrous reply from the 97-year-old young man. But I wanted nothing. Nirad Babu winked, flashed his impish smile and said 'After sundown, maybe you'd like a claret?' Soon after, he came up the stairs balancing a tray on both hands, carrying two crystal glasses of claret, a mug of some healthy hot drink for Mrs Chaudhuri, and plates of cashewnuts, potato chips, and pastry. He carefully placed the tray on the bed, pulled up a chair close to us, and we had a lovely, warm, chatty evening. That was the last I saw her. This was the first time I was visiting him since he started living alone. I needed to take someone along, to face his loneliness.

He started to talk, and talked for two hours, after which I had to leave as it was dinner time at my college. He said he had not finished what he was saying and I should come back. I said I would. And I hope I shall next year. For two hours we sat through an intense and breathless show of wit, and knowledge, memory and sensitivity, emotions and arrogance. A rare talent self-consciously presenting itself to the following generations. Nirad Babu is a great performer, a hundred per cent performer, playing to an audience almost every waking moment of his life.

Always alert, always ready to catch you on the wrong foot. So he puts you on your guard as well, keeping you tense and alert. As long as you are in front of him, he will not allow your mind to fall asleep. A silent resistance grows in you, trying not to be overpowered by this enormous show of strength. Something that he does probably to compensate for his weak physical frame. From time to time in his conversation he throws gauntlets at you, there are open challenges, which one must learn to ignore. Earlier on, I used to argue. In those days you could talk to him. In his hundredth year upon this planet, a sane man earns the right to speak at the world from above. Nirad Babu has been doing that for fifty years anyway. At last he has reached the point when it should come naturally, and the role suits him perfectly well. Today's performance was for my daughter, I supposed. For me it was as charming as always. I expected her to be mesmerized. The gentleman has the power to enthral.

He was getting ready to go to the Nehru Centre to receive the Deshikottama Award from Vishwa Bharati, and was preparing a lecture on Tagore for the occasion. His acquaintance with Tagore's works is deep and thorough, and today he was just brimming over with Tagore. As we entered his house, we heard a Tagore song being played inside. It was a romantic song for the motherland: *Ayi bhuvana-mano-mohini*. He switched it off as we entered. It was good to know he could still enjoy music, though conversation was difficult.

Once, a few years earlier, as I approached his door which was ajar, I could hear some music being played inside. Nirad Babu had asked me to listen to it carefully and tell him what was being played. I could not. I failed the test. With great glee Nirad Babu told me it was *Rule, Britannia*. It was very annoying to be tested like this, I told him, and why should I recognize *Rule, Britannia*? 'I knew you would not know it!' chuckled the jolly little gentleman. He has this habit of testing his guests' ignorance level. The first time I visited him, it was with Professor Tapan Raychaudhury. Nirad Babu still had queries about his guests. When he heard where I taught he said: 'Oh, Jadavpur University? That's a bluff.' Then, when he heard what I taught, he said: 'Oh,

Comparative Literature? That's another bluff. Buddhadeva Bose's bluff. It's nothing.' As humbly as possible I told him, 'Although I know very little of everything compared to you, there is this one thing I have been doing for fifteen years, ever since my student days, and probably know more about than you do. So please do not speak like this to me.' Undaunted, he started to recite a poem in French, completed it and asked: 'Now tell me which language is it?' It was Baudelaire. I was duly impressed by this mid-seventies memory. He too was impressed it seems, having failed to call Buddhadeva Bose's bluff. That was the day we met. We have remained friends ever since. But I still hate his habit of putting us through these tests.

I wished he would not do it this time with my daughter. He was steeped in Tagore at that moment, and started sharing his thoughts with us, talking about the women in Tagore's fiction and poetry. He also brought in Bankimchandra from time to time, quoting lines and whole paragraphs from memory. It was a great performance and I was glad I had brought my daughter along to see him. He was radiant as usual, restless and energetic bringing out books, opening up pages, pointing out exactly at which place to look for what. The big difference was that he was not jumping up and down to fetch the book, instead he was pointing them out to my daughter, he knew which book was in which pile, among those enormous piles of books on the table and on the floor.

In the midst of all this he suddenly broke out in French. I remembered another day, twenty-five years ago. French poetry. I was on my guard in an instant. I listened carefully, and was quite bewildered to hear Tagore's *Sonar Tari*—the 'Golden Boat'—recited in elegant French. As expected, he stopped and asked my daughter, 'Which language?' She looked at me with amused eyes, and said 'French' the way we talk to children. 'Whose poem?' Now was my chance to appease the child in him. 'What a beautiful translation of *Sonar Tari*. Whose translation is it?' 'Right! It's by me!' said the happy translator his face beaming with joy. This time he was unhappy to see his guests pass the ordeal. The translation was truly most competent, I would like to see it published.

Recently I was in Kishorganj, in Bangladesh, and everyone I met, started the conversation by telling me that Kishorganj had produced several great Bengali minds 'like Nirad Chaudhuri and Upendrakishore, Satyajit Ray's grandfather...' But the very first name had to be Nirad Babu's. 'Although we have a complaint against him, he was against our war of independence, he opposed our Muktiyuddha,' confessed the people of Kishorganj. Nevertheless they loved him for what he was, and shared his international glory. Nirad Babu always identifies himself as a boy from Kishorganj first, then a Bengali intellectual from Calcutta, and lastly an Indian. I wanted to tell him about the people of Kishorganj. But in those two word-filled and emotion-filled hours all I could say was what he wanted to hear. About the French translation of Tagore.

That evening Nirad Babu talked a great deal about Mrs Chaudhuri, and showed us several of her photographs at different ages. 'She walked alone by the river early in the mornings. It was absolutely safe, it is not possible in Oxford any longer. It is a dangerous place for women during twilight hours not to speak of the dark. England is no place for civilized people anymore, it is full of sex and violence. I would not want my grandchildren to grow up here, or even to be educated here. I have sent my granddaughter back to India for her studies.' I felt sad, but didn't have the heart to tell him that today's India was just as unsafe. Let him imagine a saner, safer world back home. A *Bhuvana mana-mohini* homeland that he has left behind and to which he can return no more, after he enters his second century.

A happy hundredth birthday, Meshomoshai, and our loving *pranam* in jeans and *saris.*

NIRAD BABU RECALLED

William Radice

I first heard about Nirad C. Chaudhuri in 1969, when I taught for a few months at the Lawrence School, Sanawar (Simla Hills), between leaving school and going to university. The School's bursar—'Buster' Manley, ex-Indian police, married to an Indian—discussed him with me one day when we went out for a walk; maybe I mentioned him first, having come across his *Continent of Circe* in the school library. I am afraid my memory is not as good as Nirad Babu's, and all I really remember about the discussion was that I learnt that 'Nirad' was pronounced 'Nirode'. Buster was a good linguist—spoke excellent Hindi—and clearly knew something about the vagaries of Bengali pronunciation.

During those months in India I visited Calcutta, and was specially intrigued by the astonishing Marble Palace. The films of

Satyajit Ray had already made a deep impression on me in my mid-teens; I think a growing awareness of Nirad Babu through his books and through articles about him was a significant influence on my decision to learn Bengali after I finished my English degree at Oxford. It was the hybrid culture of the nineteenth-century Bengal Renaissance that particularly fascinated me. Nirad was a living representative of it. Not that I got very far, at that stage, with his masterpiece, *The Autobiography of an Unknown Indian*, published in the year I was born (1951). It is not a book for young people. Every year I religiously place it on reading-lists at the School for Oriental and African Studies (SOAS), but hardly any student reads it right through. I myself only read it complete, and with great pleasure and admiration, about six years ago.

While I was a student at Oxford, I became marginally involved in the Critical Society—an undergraduate society that invited prominent *literateurs* to give talks. In 1970 Sukanta Chaudhuri came up to University College, to read English. I met him at the 'Fresher's Fair', when new undergraduates are introduced to Oxford's rich array of clubs and societies. I think I was there to 'sell' the Critical Society. Nirad Babu had recently come to live in Oxford, and had been in the news. I must have mentioned him to Sukanta, for I remember him saying guardedly that Nirad was 'a bit of an exhibitionist'—which made me realize how complex his relationship was with his countrymen. Since then I have encountered, among Bengalis, every shade of opinion of him, from the near apoplexy of my Bengali teacher Tarapada Mukherjee at the mention of his name ('I don't believe that Nirad Chaudhuri is capable of understanding the *first thing* about Tagore') to warm pride and affection.

In 1970 or 1971, Nirad Babu gave a talk to the Critical Society. He will be able to give the exact date—from his files, if not from his unrivalled memory—for in January 1990 he wrote to me:

> I have to apologize to you for not thanking you earlier for your letter and your book of translations from Tagore.
>
> Before I give my excuses, I would tell you that I

> perfectly remember the misadventure at the back door of our Wheatley house, the dinner at the Union; the talk, and the bumptious Bengali. Indeed, some time ago, looking through my old papers, I came upon a letter from you to me.

The 'misadventure' at the Wheatley house was excruciatingly embarrassing at the time, comical in retrospect. Somehow, in the dark, I and the one or two others who had gone there to fetch him missed the front door of the house. We knocked instead at the glass-panelled back door, through which we could clearly see Nirad Babu in the kitchen, talking to his wife. Either we knocked too timidly—or maybe we pressed a bell that wasn't working properly; but somehow we had the firm impression that Nirad had indeed heard us, but would only come when he was ready. So we stood there, waiting and waiting, and watching him through the panel. He meanwhile was waiting for us. Eventually he saw us, or perhaps we plucked up courage to knock again, and I daresay he made light of our mistake but the evening had not got off to a very good start. Dinner at the Union was initially not much easier. The food was ample in quantity but probably mediocre in quality, for I remember Nirad Babu eating little and saying that he was 'a *gourmet* not a *gourmand*'. It was difficult to raise any topic of conversation, without having one's ignorance mercilessly exposed; history, literature, languages—whatever, the subject, he knew far more about it than we did; but he paraded his knowledge in a spirit of joyous curiosity so infectious that it gradually dispelled our discomfiture, helped no doubt by the wine. (My wife Elizabeth, who was there too, says that she remembers that he ordered the most expensive wine on the list.) By the time we moved on to a room—in Balliol?—for the talk, we were merrily ready for anything, however surreal or bizarre. I remember perhaps three things about the talk. One was that Nirad said he didn't believe in dialogue, and that Plato's dialogues were in fact the greatest monologues every written. The second was that he firmly believed that empires were forces for civilization, which is why he dedicated his *Autobiography of an Unknown*

Indian to the British Raj. Thirdly, I remember how someone in the audience decided to take issue with him. Provoked either by the famous words of the dedication, which Nirad read out with characteristic panache,* or something he had said about Bengalis, his challenger began (in the fruitiest of Oxford accents), 'But I am a Bengali . . .' at which Nirad shrieked, 'Counter-lecture, counter-lecture' and gleefully offered him the podium. I have no idea how the evening was eventually salvaged from the ensuing chaos.

In 1979 my wife and I moved from London to Oxford, so that I could start work on my D.Phil on Michael Madhusudan Datta. In all the twelve years that we lived there, I never met Nirad Babu, though I saw him once from a bus, walking briskly up the Banbury Road, bobbing his head in typical bird-like fashion. The sight of him made me recall something I'd read in an interview with him in the Calcutta magazine *Desh*, about the heads of girls turning when he walked along Oxford's streets. There were plenty of occasions when I could have met him: gatherings of Oxford Bengalis or India-specialists, the occasional talk or seminar that he gave. Or I could have simply picked up the phone and asked if I could visit him. But somehow our paths never crossed. Perhaps I was shy, or too nervous about how he would regard my work on Bengali and in particular my translations of Tagore. In the end, towards the end of 1989, I plucked up courage and sent him a new reprint of my Penguin *Selected Poems of Tagore.* It was in response to that that he wrote me the letter quoted above, and another a bit later on. He was kind about my work, but sceptical about all translations of poetry:

> I have not yet read them through, but I can say that it's a relief to find English translations of Tagore's poems, instead of Bengali in Roman typography.
>
> But my objection is generally to all translations of poetry. I never read any translations of French poetry.

---

* *To the memory of the British Empire in India which conferred subjecthood on us but withheld citizenship; to which yet every one of us threw out the challenge* Civis Britannicus Sum *because, all that was good and living within us was made, shaped and quickened by the same British rule.*

> In regard to Tagore, the difficulties increase from poem to poem—some can be given approximate English versions, some not at all...

He objected to my translation of *Badhu* (the title of a well-known poem in *Manasi*, 1890) as 'bride':

> . . . *Badhu* in Bengali has never been 'bride'—bride in Bengal (perhaps all over India) ceases to exist with the end of the wedding night. Then she becomes *badhu* or *bau*. Unfortunately there is no English word for it, and your falling back on 'Bride' is understood linguistically, but not socially or psychologically. In French *badhu* has been translated as *la jeune mariée*, but *mariée* in French means both a 'bride' and a 'young wife'.

I argued in return—and would still argue—that 'bride' is the only English word that would convey to the non-Indian reader the extreme youth of the girl in the poem. But I never expected to convince Nirad Babu that there was any point in translating Tagore, and was content and relieved that he did not, it seemed, scorn my efforts totally.

Two years later, when I did, in the end, visit Nirad Babu at his home in North Oxford, I realized that I had been foolish to be so terrified of his reaction. I had organized a series of seminars at SOAS on 'Great Bengalis' (Tagore, Vidyasagar, Bankim *et al*), and I had been hoping to invite Nirad Babu himself as a living specimen of the breed. He graciously declined, on grounds of deteriorating eyesight. I said that instead, I and Dr Ranjana Ash would discuss his book *Atmaghati Rabindranath* (1992); we would record the discussion, and I would bring the recording and play it to him. He replied that he wasn't interested in the recording (he didn't believe that an author had any right 'to object to or for that matter even endorse publicly anything said or written about him'), but would be very pleased if I came to see him anyway.

On a beautiful November day—fallen leaves still blowing about on the pavements—I found myself ringing his doorbell. No confusion about the door this time! By then my wife, our two daughters and I had left Oxford, to make my wife's grandfather's house in Northumberland our main home, with a tiny flat in London so that I could continue to lecture at SOAS. North Oxford was looking at its best, and I felt rather nostalgic and melancholy, wondering why we had moved so dramatically away from our Oxford roots. But as soon as Nirad Babu opened the door I felt cheered: the move had given the visit more significance, made it more of a pilgrimage. It was as though part of me had been with Nirad Babu all the time I had lived in Oxford, and it was only now that I had moved physically away that I could turn my mental connection with him into a physical meeting. He greeted me as an old friend, saying that the last time we had met I had been a student, and now I was a 'professor' (just a humble lecturer, actually, but perhaps he was slipping into Indian usage).

There are many things I remember about our meeting, but certain details remain particularly vivid, shining in my memory like the November sunshine. The string quartet (Haydn?) that was playing on the gramophone when I arrived, and the almost balletic grace with which Nirad Babu (dressed in *Panjabi* and pyjamas this time, not suit and tie) took the needle off the record, the gesture of his arm matching the phrasing of the music. The easy and natural way in which he spoke to me in a mixture of Bengali and English, as he would to a Bengali visitor. (That was another thing that had worried me: whether he would want to speak to me in Bengali at all.) Our vigorous discussion about the differences between *chalit bhasha* (standard 'colloquial' Bengali) and the sonorous *sadhu bhasha* that Nirad Babu—uniquely among living Bengali writers—still writes. (I understood him to say that the combination of highly Sanskritic vocabulary with *chalit* pronouns and verb forms—as in most academic Bengali writing today—produces an effect as indecorous to his ear as a mixture of formal, academic language with colloquial abbreviations—I'm, can't etc.—would be in English.) I remember too the insight he gave me into the huge, perfectionist effort behind his lapidary

English style, how even now he would spend many hours checking in the dictionary words he had used in a rapidly written first draft. The way, all the while, he kept tapping me on the arm or shoulder, bird-like again, his finger jabbing like a bird's beak. The arrival, during our meeting, of a man from the local garden centre, with a selection of flower seeds that Nirad Babu had ordered. The expertise and enthusiasm with which he examined the seed packets; his friendly conversation with the seed-man; the flamboyant elegance with which he wrote out a cheque with a large fountain pen. A constant impression of grace, agility, energy, nimbleness, fun, wit, *joie de vivre* . . .

There are other things I wish I had discussed with him, had I had longer and had come better prepared. I should like, for example, to have talked to him more about my family connections with India. In one of his letters to me he wrote:

> I was very much interested to learn that your family had a long association with India (which province?). Since your family has been domiciled in England for a long time, how does it happen that the surname is still pronounced in the Italian way (as I am told), and has not been Anglicized as simple 'Radiss? and how was it pronounced in India?

In Tagore's essay *Raja o praja* (*Rabindrarachanabali* Vol. 10, p. 542; first published in *Sadhana, Shraban*, B.S. 1301), he would find an answer to that last question, for there is a reference there to my grandfather, Charles Albert Radice, who was in the Indian Civil Service (ICS) in Bengal from 1890 to 1915. The essay begins with the words '*Sibhiliyan Radici-saheb...*', indicating that the name was correctly pronounced in India, albeit with a hard English 'd' rather than a soft dental Italian sound. It was the late Subhendusekhar Mukhopadhyay, editor of the West Bengal Government edition of Tagore's works (1980), who first drew my attention to this small but interesting Radice-Tagore link, ninety-one years before my *Selected Poems of Tagore* was published. Tagore refers to the public reprimand and demotion of my grandfather, by the Lieutenant Governor, *McDonell-Saheb*, for illegally insulting and harassing a *zamindar* in Orissa. This was apparently greeted with public jubilation (*ananda*) in Bengal: and there was equally intense public distress (*shok*) when McDonell's successor, *Eliot-saheb*, reinstated my grandfather after a respectable interval. Tagore makes the thoroughly valid point that in fact, under colonial rule, the subject people of India (*praja*) knew very little about what their rulers were really thinking. A public admission of fault might conceal a very different attitude among the rulers (*raja*) themselves. There would only be real cause for *ananda* in India when the people themselves stood up for justice, and protested at its infringement by their rulers. In Tagore's own words (my translation):

> When we are able to forget the poisonous lessons of a long-established servitude to a foreign ruler, when we no longer helplessly and silently resign ourselves to the unjust behaviour of the powerful as if it were decreed by fate, when we know that to strive against injustice is our duty—even when it comes to nought—and when we do not flinch from any suffering or self-sacrifice we may thereby endure, then the day will have arrived when we shall have true cause for jubilation...

When Subhendu Babu told me—in December 1983—about this essay, I immediately wrote to my great-uncle, Fulke Rosavo Radice, Charles' youngest brother, author of an 800-page history of the Radice family, and almost as prodigious in memory and age as Nirad Babu himself. (Fulke died in 1987, at the age of ninety-nine.) He was an amateurish historian in that he put into his history every bit of information he could find about the family, however trivial, except for incidents that might reflect badly on us: hence his omission of my grandfather's *faux pas*. His reply to my letter tellingly confirms Tagore's insight: the demotion was indeed a public, face-saving exercise, and did not represent the Lieutenant Governor's personal views:

> Please forgive a belated reply with good wishes to all your family. As it happens I can say to you that I have quite a good recollection of the incident you refer to in your letter. I remember my Mamma explaining it either to a cousin or to a friend. In 1896 I was only eight years old but I remember the incident. According to my Mamma, the Radice in question was my second brother Charlie who was only about twenty-nine. According to my Mamma Adele's account Charlie ought to have ordered the police to arrest the landlord, but did it himself, which was wrong, and led to his being reprimanded by the Lieutenant Governor, Sir Anthony McDonell. My and Charlie's Papa wrote to Sir A.P., as he was known, on behalf of Charlie and Sir A.P. said in return that Charlie's error was one of zeal. He was entitled to order the landlord to be arrested but had no authority to carry out the arrest himself in person, as he did, and received a reprimand in consequence. Sir A.P. replied in those terms to Papa and rather praised Charlie, though he had been guilty of an error in law. I don't know if we have Sir A.P.'s letter still in the family papers. I have had no time yet to look them up.'*

There are other Radice-Indian connections that would interest Nirad Babu. Charlie's eldest brother Evasio ('Vasi') was also in the ICS, is still remembered—so I am told—by a 'Radice Prize for Hindi' at a college in Benares, and until Independence had a

* *The Radice family papers are now kept in the library of Manchester College, Oxford. It seemed an appropriate place to put them, when I discovered there were already letters from my great-great grandmother Maria (née Hutton) in the Martineau family papers. My great-great grandfather, Evasio Radice, who came to Britain as a political exile from Piedmont in 1821, became friendly with the (Unitarian) Martineau family, and his wife kept in touch with them after his death in Genoa in 1855. Manchester College, which has a Unitarian foundation, also has connections with Tagore (he gave his lectures on* The Religion of Man *there in 1930), and the Tagore family through the Brahmo Samaj—has connections with Unitarianism.*

street named after him in Lucknow.+ 'Radice & Co. (India Ltd.),' an engineering firm founded by William Italo Archibald Radice ('Willie'), another of Charlie's brothers, was still to be found, a few years ago, in the Calcutta telephone book. My father's elder brother Peter was in the ICS until 1949, and then settled in the (Channel) island of Alderney, where I spent many a childhood holiday and heard much about India from him and his (German) wife Margaret. They were my favourite uncle and aunt. In the same envelope in which I keep Nirad Babu's letters I have a letter from Peter which is mainly about him. He had earlier written to me about *Thy Hand, Great Anarch!*, which he had read with keen interest, having lived through the events that Nirad describes.

All these matters could, I am sure, be profitably discussed with Nirad Babu. I may never do so, but one thing is for sure: if I ever try to research my family's connections with India in more detail—looking up the newspaper reports, say, that must have prompted Tagore's essay—Nirad C. Chaudhuri's books will help me perhaps more than any others to understand the historical context.

I have not written about those books in this essay, knowing that other contributors to this volume will certainly do so. But I should like to say that I consider them to be great books, that will be read and re-read through the generations. For me, pp.xxi-xxiii of the introduction to *Thy Hand, Great Anarch*! (expanded in the Epilogue, *Credo ut Intelligam*) confirm and partly explain his greatness as a writer, and strike a deeply personal chord with me, since I myself have had cause to thank 'a great mercy immanent in the universe which takes care precisely of those who are least fit to take care of themselves.' But that is another story, and it would not be right for me to tell it until I have lived at least as half as many years as Nirad Babu.

+Or was it in Benares? Both are recalled by different family members. Maybe someone in India will be able to verify.

'WE SAY DESH' : THE OTHER NIRAD BABU

Meenakshi Mukherjee

I dialled the number with much trepidation. Having always been in great awe of his erudition, and apprehensive of his famous eccentricities, I would never have had the temerity to initiate a conversation with the legendary Nirad C. Chaudhuri without being prodded by someone else. The push came from my friend Alastair Niven who was incredulous that in spite of being a Bangla-speaking Indian I had never met this monument of unaging intellect. Alastair and I were together in London for a jury meeting of some literary award, and he insisted that I make a special pilgrimage to Oxford to fill up this unseemly lacuna in my life by doing a proper *darshan*. 'But what shall I say to him?' I asked. I was diffident, reluctant to treat a human being as if he was the Taj Mahal or the Statue of Liberty. 'There is no need for you to say anything. He will do the talking,' Alastair egged me on and, when he discovered that I was in any case going to Oxford that weekend to meet a friend, there was no holding him back. Next morning he called to inform me that he had already told Mr Chaudhuri about my desire to meet him.

This was 1989, long past the days of my youthful enthusiasm when I might have ardently 'desired' to meet a writer. By now I was quite content to read a writer and not to have to make his acquaintance. But there being no decent way of backing out any more, I called the number Alastair had given me. Nirad Babu picked up the phone himself. I mentioned my name and began very hesitantly in Bangla—'You don't know me, but . . .' 'I know you. I have met you', he interrupted very firmly. I could not imagine where or how. 'At a conference called "The Eye of the Beholder" organized by the Commonwealth Institute in London in 1982'; he gave me the date and place precisely.

It was quite incredible. Indeed there had been such a conference held in the era when we were assaulting European countries with our Festivals, quite a few years before Indian Writers in English became our major selling commodity. So much had changed since then that it all seemed like a long time ago. The conference had turned out to be a small and lively one and to me the star participant was young Salman Rushdie, a recent winner of the Booker Prize, sharp and energetic, still relatively untouched by the glare of media attention, quite distant from the controversy that would later change his life. Nobody could have thought then that this vibrant young man would one day turn into a staid literary oracle, pronouncing judgment on Indian books he has never read. But another writer present at the same conference was already doing that. To this day I remember Anita Desai's astounding statement made on this occasion which has since been preserved in cold print—' . . . there is very little fiction written by women in India. The few novels that have been written are for the most part in English'. [1]

The conference was memorable for many other reasons. In response to Raja Rao's philosophical statements about Indian tradition—equated almost wholly with the Brahmanic heritage (to

Raja Rao knowing of Sanskrit was synonymous with being an Indian)—and Professor C.D. Narasimhaiah's assertion that despite having components of 'Buddhist, Jain, Parsi, Christian, Sikh and Mughal', Indian culture is 'predominantly Hindu', the younger writers intervened with sprightly combativeness. It was pointed out by them that the women and the lower castes never had access to Sanskrit and a homogenization of India excludes all minorities. The range of participants included the young and old, famous and not so famous, resident Indians like us and our diasporic cousins. On the one hand there were the established writers like Mulk Raj Anand, Raja Rao and Anita Desai. On the other hand there were writers like Arun Kolhatkar, Gieve Patel, Faroukh Dhondy and the perpetually angry Sasthi Brata, not to speak of the irreverent Rushdie. There was a freshness in the debate at that point. The first volume of *Subaltern Studies* had been published only that year and its discourse had still not percolated down to all academic and literary spheres to make the questions of minority and marginality routinely central in conference interventions. The word 'post-colonial' had not yet gained currency and the political visibility of BJP and VHP was still an event in the future. The cut and thrust of the opposing viewpoints had not yet congealed into a predictable rhetoric. There was a ring of individually thought out conviction in the opinions expressed which I had found most stimulating.

The reason I did not think of Nirad C. Chaudhuri in connection with this conference was that he was not present for any of these scintillating dialogues. He came from Oxford for the first session to deliver his inaugural address in the evening and went back the same night. Even though I remembered his lecture vividly, I did not connect it with the conference. It was a separate and spectacular performance where he traced the most unexpected and original connections between the English language and Indian culture with none of the ostrich-like complacency displayed by some Indo-Anglian writers who claimed that there was hardly a literary culture in India other than in English. Even at that time I was aware of Nirad Chaudhuri's double persona—as a writer in English and a writer in Bangla—and had a special admiration for him because of this, though I knew he preferred to keep these identities separate. That evening he had come as a writer in English, armed with several exhibits—three textbooks he had studied in Kishorganj High School in 1908; a Bangla almanac or *panjika* of 1905 which, apart from prescribing exact dates and moments propitious for performing *pujas*, eating of pumpkins and co-habiting with one's wife, also provided model letters to be written in English; an Intermediate textbook of Calcutta University with an essay on Xenophon by Alexander Grant, and a painting by Romney showing an infant Shakespeare 'attended by Nature and the Passions' found at one time in Shakespeare-adoring Bengali homes. He made dramatic use of these props to situate in history his own evolving relationship with English culture, keeping us spellbound for an hour. He went back to Oxford the same night, not to return for the rest of the conference. He was well past eighty and it was not expected that he would sit through the entire proceedings. As with most inaugural speeches, his talk was not followed by a question-answer session nor did he have, as far as I recall, any informal interaction with the other participants of the conference.

I asked him on telephone how he could have remembered me because I did not have a chance to speak to him on that occasion. 'I have a habit of noticing women, specially young women', he said impishly. Since we were conversing in Bangla, the words he used were '*yuvati ramani*', which have an erotic charge, absent in its bland English equivalent. I was amused. 'In that case you do not really remember me, because I am not a *yuvati ramani*', I said. 'Now that I have crossed eighty all women look *yuvati* to me': his retort silenced me.

We arranged to meet the next evening. I had suggested five o'clock, but he insisted on four-fifteen. My husband also happened to be in London, and we had both been invited for dinner at the house of our friends Trilokesh and Margaret who lived in Oxford those days. We decided to perform the *darshan* together before going on to their place, even though Trilokesh, when he heard of our plan, warned my husband to keep a very low profile, because Nirad Babu according to him, had a well-known aversion to tall men, and those above six feet were a special anathema. We never found out if Trilokesh was right, but we did notice that Sujit was pointedly offered the lowest chair in the living room by our host, while he sat on a fairly high one, presumably his usual seat. I could sit anywhere I liked. But he was affable and charming to both of us alike and kept us riveted for nearly two hours with his reflections on life and literature in Bangla, unadulterated by a single English word. He took me to task for using the word 'India' inadvertently in one of my brief interjections—'We do not say India, we say *desh*', he admonished me.

He has proclaimed many times in his writing his intolerance of slip-shod mixing of ingredients in sartorial, gastronomic and language practices. He grew up and lived in an age when hybridity was still a negative word and his standards of purity continue to be high indeed. Even in his most recent book, written in his hundredth year (*Three Horsemen of the Apocalypse*), he has measured the decline of Bengali culture along the rising popularity graph of *idli-vada* and Chinese food. Another cause of lament is the Bengali's abandonment of the elegant *dhoti-kurta* in favour of 'capricious' and tasteless assortments of clothing items, the final vulgarity being the adoption, almost as national dress, of T-shirts with alien logos.[2] On that December evening of 1989, he welcomed us in a *dhoti* and a brown flannel *kurta* of the kind commonly seen in our childhood, but gone out of use in recent decades. He insisted on bringing in the tea-trolley himself, graciously declining my attempts to help him: 'Guests who have come to our house for the first time are not allowed to do any work'. Mrs Chaudhuri sat with us and participated in the conversation, but her arthritis kept her confined to a wheel chair.

It was so easy to sit back and listen to him that I soon forgot my earlier apprehensions. He particularly warmed to us when he found that we knew very closely his contemporary from Calcutta University—Sudhanshu Kumar Das who retired as a judge of the Supreme Court of India in 1963—another admirable human being who continued to be interested in books, ideas and people right until his death in 1994 in Delhi. Perhaps that 1898 model of human beings was very special, not repeated since then. Nirad

Babu also probed our Patna background and came up with names of people like Rangin Haldar who he knew in his youth. All went well until at one point I opened my mouth a bit too wide and put my foot into it.

In response to his query about how long we were going to be in London, I said perhaps a week or ten days more, because I had to do some reading in the British Museum. 'What do you want to read?' he asked, fixing me with a stare. At that time I was writing a monograph on Jane Austen for the Macmillan Women Writers Series, and had set upon myself the task of reading all the late eighteenth-century bestsellers in England that young Jane might have read herself—books either mentioned or obliquely referred to in her novels. This seemed to interest him. 'You are writing a book on Jane Austen! How well have you read her own novels?' he challenged me. 'Fairly well, I think', I said guardedly, taking courage from the fact that Jane Austen, like E.M. Forster, was one of the few English novelists whose complete works could be read thoroughly even without making it a lifetime occupation. Mrs Chaudhuri, who seemed to be an amused observer of her husband's idiosyncrasies, at this point exclaimed with a smile directed at me: 'Now you have got yourself into trouble!' I did not know at that time that Jane Austen was one of Nirad Babu's favourite writers and he read a few pages from her novels almost every night.

What followed was a close interrogation of my textual knowledge of the six Jane Austen novels in which examination, I must confess I barely managed a B grade. It involved remembering details of Darcy's clothing on specific occasions, knowing the meaning of certain colours of British heraldry, the distance between Hunsford and Longbourne, the number of horses used for drawing different kinds of carriages and the like. The one that completely floored me had to do with the size of Fanny Price's room in the attic in Mansfield Park. To this day I cannot figure out how he worked it out. As he explained to me it had something to do with the space taken up by Fanny's bookshelf which he calculated by locating the original edition of each book mentioned and adding up their dimensions. I was not convinced, because I did not think all the books Fanny read were mentioned in the novel, but discretion seemed to be the better part of valour. He too took pity on me after a while and decided to let me off the hook, promising to send me a piece on Jane Austen he had written for the *Times Literary Supplement.* A few days later in London I did receive the promised piece in a packet along with a pen carefully wrapped in cotton wool which I had left behind in Nirad Babu's house.

*

That was eight years ago. I have often wondered since then, specially while reading Nirad Babu's Bangla work, when he upbraided me about my use of English and asked me to say *desh*, was he really giving me an equivalent of 'India'? Earlier I had carelessly believed that his Bangla writing was an off-shoot of his English work, similar in attitude, content and range, if not in style. His use of the *sadhu bhasha* verb forms certainly set him apart from Bangla writers of today as being deliberately old-fashioned, and he has never concealed his contempt for the more informal version of the language as it is written today. Since English does not have a similar grammatical marker to set apart old and new usages, he does not stand out from contemporary English writers in so obvious a manner, even though other stylistic features may remind the reader of his vintage. But this is only a superficial difference. I am beginning to believe that his agenda and objectives are fundamentally different when he is writing in English and in Bangla.

Language can play strange tricks with our perceptions and self-images. Who knows it better than Nirad Babu who had pointed out several anomalous examples of this in the inaugural speech mentioned above.[3] But he seems to have been an unconscious prey to these paradoxes himself. While in his English autobiography in 1951 he had identified himself as an 'Unknown Indian', in a Bengali piece he rejected this identity emphatically. He declared: 'I project myself as a Bengali, never as an Indian. The more recent appellation *"Asian"* I cannot even dream of using.' [4] He pre-empts possible charges of inconsistency by pleading amnesia in another essay *Akshamer Kshamata* (The Power of the Powerless): 'When I write in English I completely forget that I know Bangla; similarly while writing Bangla I do not remember knowing any English'. [5]

Such overstatements are familiar features of his style and need not be taken literally. But English and Bangla do provide him with different perspectives and two target audiences, provoking him to assume contradictory positions. In his recent English book he claims to have 'a complete knowledge of Bengal', [6] but only two years ago in a Bangla essay he had confessed that after he left Calcutta for Delhi in 1942, he has hardly had any contact with Bengal, and 'since 1970 I have been in Oxford, I have not been back even once. Thus I have no direct knowledge of Bengali life.' [7] Such contradictions seem fairly frequent when his works in two different languages are read side by side.

*

Shri Nirad Chandra Chaudhuri (in Bangla he always uses this complete form) published his first full-length book *Bangali Jibane Ramani* (Women in Bengali Life) in 1968, stating in the Preface: 'At the age of fifty I wrote my first English book; at the age of seventy this is my first in Bangla. I thought it was late for English; I shudder to think how late it is for Bangla' [8]. It was not as if he was writing in Bangla for the first time, because he was part of a literary coterie in Calcutta in his youth, and in 1927-28 served as the editor of the journal *Shanibarer Chithi* (The Saturday Letter), well known for its scathing critical pieces and acerbic wit. Among his closest friends was Bibhutibhushan Bandyopadhyay, known outside Bengal mainly as the author of *Pather Panchali*, and Chaudhuri has written about this friendship several times, including in *Thy Hand, Great Anarch*! Later, Nirad Babu had worked for another well-known Bangla journal *Probashi* in 1932. But indeed, after he left Calcutta in 1942, he was out of touch for thirty years and returned to Bangla first with long essays in the weekly *Desh* in the mid-sixties, to be followed by this controversial book in 1968, written at the insistence of a literary friend of his youth, Gajendra Kumar Mitra, who had by this time turned publisher.

Bangali Jibane Ramani presented a unique thesis about the role of English literature in the evolution of *kama* (physical desire) into *prem* (romantic love) in nineteenth-century Bengali life. This was a 300-page elaboration of a point he had briefly made in *A Passage to England*: 'We in Bengal began to deal with love from a literary end. That is to say it was transferred to Bengali literature from English literature, and then taken over from literature to life. As a result of this double transplantation, the plant remains delicate and a hothouse atmosphere is needed for its survival.'[9] In *Bangali Jibane Ramani* he marshalls an impressive array of evidences to prove his thesis not only from literary texts in Sanskrit and Bangla (from Bhavabhuti, Kalidasa and Jaidev to Bharatchandra, Chandidas, Bankimchandra and Rabindranath) but from less respectable sources as well: bawdy wedding songs, rustic doggerels, and snippets of women's conversations remembered from his rural childhood, where parts of the body were referred to in a diction that still exists in crude speech but rarely finds its way into print. Since the time Nirad Babu mischievously introduced the gross vocabulary of popular culture in a serious discourse on nineteenth-century Bengal, detailed research has been done in this field, particularly by Sumanta Banerjee [10] who demonstrates how this 'low' culture, often associated with women, was a source of embarrassment for the English educated enlightened Bengali male. It has to be said for Nirad Chaudhuri's Bangla writing, he constantly reminds his readers that behind the much-discussed *bhadralok* way of life there was a strong popular culture vibrant in its crude energy.

His peppering of learned essays with Bangla equivalents of four-letter words had the desired effect of outraging Bengali readers into writing long irate letters to the editor when some earlier versions of the book appeared in *Desh*. In fact, he remained a controversial writer in Bangla for a long time, a large number of readers strongly taking the rather simplistic position that as a blind admirer of everything Western, Chaudhuri has made a career out of debunking India and particularly Bengal. Another popular myth that he belittles Rabindranath Tagore also does not bear close scrutiny, because his range of reading in Tagore is amazing and his anguish at the blind iconization of the poet by the Bengalis who hardly know his work has to be taken seriously. In fact his long essay *Rabindranather Aparahna* (The Afternoon of Rabindranath) about the loneliness of the poet who received the Nobel Prize is one of his most moving pieces of writing in which he sees this prize as casting a dark shadow of false fame over Rabindranath's true achievement. [11] For many years anything written by Nirad Babu in *Desh*—a journal well-known for its lively correspondence columns—was followed by rejoinders and attacks lasting for months. Of late, however, perhaps in deference to his age, or because of a growing mellowness of his own tone, the controversy seems to have ebbed somewhat.

Much of his controversial status in Bangla is, of course, of his own seeking. His Bangla corpus which may be seen as an almost continuous reflection on Bengali life, literature and history, segmented in several books and long essays, (one of his books, incidentally, is called *Atmaghati Bangali*, 1988 or The Suicidal Bengali), is also a ceaseless introspection on his own love-hate relationship with his origins, and by varying the tropes in describing the tension he brings to bear new perspectives on the topic. At one point he thinks of Bengal as a stagnant lagoon and decides to abandon it to sail on the open ocean. 'A rupture happened between me and life and society in Bengal which continues even today. I am moving and will continue to move. They are static.' [12] At another place he uses the Tagore story *Streer Patra* (Letter from a Wife, 1914) as a metaphor for his feelings towards Bengal. When Mrinal, the rebellious second daughter-in-law of a joint family in Calcutta escaped from the claustrophobic household to come face to face with the sky and the sea, she realized how confined her earlier life and been. Referring to this Nirad Chaudhuri writes: 'Like Mrinal I can now say, "Where are your walls of masonry now, where are the barbed wire fences made up of rules and prohibitions? Your insults and humiliations cannot keep me imprisoned any more . . . . You had kept me concealed in the gloom of your mindless routine. Only after coming outside I can see myself in my full glory".'[13] Elsewhere he compares his creative freedom after coming out of Bengal with the dance of Kipling's Kaa after his change of skin (*The Jungle Book*), which the monkeys watched with hypnotized fascination. 'The educated Bengali has not been able to take his eyes off my dancing since 1951, and will not be able to, as long as I am alive'.[14]

Yet he feels the need to carry on a dialogue with the people he has rejected, and keeps providing various justifications for renewing his career in Bangla so late in life. 'Bengalis look at their own people writing in English in the same way they respond to wild animals performing in a circus—not as a natural act but as tricks learnt through rigorous discipline. The more intricate the act the more they applaud; this writing may appeal to their head, but it does not touch the heart'[15]. Writing in Bangla, evidently, is the only way to touch their heart. At another place he declares that he has no desire to be known as a writer in Bangla: 'The intention is not to achieve literary fame, but merely to carry on a conversation with the Bengali people about their history and religion. As long as they listen to me I do not care if I am recognized as a writer'.[16] In yet another place he confesses: 'I have realized I cannot reach the educated Bengalis today through my English writing. Firstly, they have lost the habit of reading English. They do not read easily and therefore they do not enjoy what they read. Secondly, most Bengali readers no longer have the ability to appreciate the kind of English that British publishers find acceptable. Perhaps they understand half the meaning, but the resonance and significance of the other half is lost to them. The English that is current in England is thus only partially accessible to the Bengali. Then why write in English for them? In the present reduced state of the Bengali people, if anyone has anything to say to them, it should be conveyed in a language they can comprehend.'[17]

True to his quirky temperament, after having made these contradictory statements—one appealing to the heart, and the other arrogant and condescending—he goes on to write books and essays that hardly need these declarations. In a disarming autobiographical piece—perhaps meant to be in the mode of Rousseau or St. Augustine—he confesses his own meanness and vulnerability, his profligacy, his neglect of work, his inordinate delight at having received a generous dowry, his self-indulgence and vanity. He describes amusingly how he never paid for the dentures he got made before getting married and how on his wedding night he had the presumption to ask his bride if she could spell Beethoven. But at the end of this candid and human story he suddenly remembers his agenda and holds forth on how the entire narrative is written for the benefit of the defeated Bengali people so that they too can learn how to succeed in life.

Shri Nirad Chandra Chaudhuri sought to bid farewell to his second career in 1996 by writing his 'Last Words to the Bengali People'.[18] But one hopes that he will live long enough to write a post-script to it in which he will clarify at least one slippage of concepts between his two languages. He taught me to say *desh* for homeland which is presumably India when he writes in English, but must it narrow down to a non-existent Bengal whenever he takes up his crusade in his mother tongue?

(All English translations from Nirad Chaudhuri's Bangla writing have been done by the author.)

Chapter Notes

1. Anita Desai, 'India Women Writers' in *The Eye of the Beholder: Indian Writing in English*. London: 1983, p. 54
2. Quoted from the extract in *India Today* (July 28, 1997) from *Three Horsemen of the New Apocalypse*. p. 90.
3. For example, he mentioned a line in a model letter in English published in a 1905 almanac where an Indian father is supposed to be writing to his son: 'Your mother, like myself feels aggrieved that you have asked for an additional allowance.' Nirad C. Chaudhuri's comment is: '. . . A Hindu would not write "Your mother and I", but "I and your mother". We could not write in English without changing mentally.' *The Eye of the Beholder*, p. 10

4. *Bangalir Kachhe Aamar Shesh Katha*, *Desh* (Sharadiya), 1402, p. 137.
5. *Akshamer Kshamata*, *Desh* (Sharadiya), 1400, p. 55.
6. *India Today*, July 28, 1997, p. 90.
7. *Bangalir Kachhe Aamar Shesh Katha*, *Desh* (Sharadiya), 1402, p. 132.
8. Preface to *Bangali Jibane Ramani*, Calcutta: 1968, p. 10.
9. *A Passage to England*, London: 1959, p. 115-16.
10. 'Marginalization of Women's Popular Culture in Nineteenth Century Bengal' in *Recasting Women*, ed. Kumkum Sangari and Sudesh Vaid, New Delhi: 1989.
11. *Rabindranather Aparahna*, *Desh* (Sharadiya), 1398, p. 158.
12. *Akshamer Kshamata* p. 63.
13. *Bangalir Kachhe Aamar Shesh Katha*, p. 134.
14. *Ibid*
15. *Akshamer Kshamata*, p. 55.
16. Preface to *Bangali Jibane Ramani*, p. 15.
17. *Ibid*, p. 14.
18. *Bangalir Kachhe Aamar Shesh Katha*, *Desh* (Sharadiya), 1402.

NIRAD C. CHAUDHURI : SCHOLAR AND ICONOCLAST

K. Natwar-Singh

In the garden of his house in Oxford the leaves are beginning to fall. While he may not have followed Yeats to 'spit into the face of time . . .', he has certainly defied it. For Nirad C. Chaudhuri there has been no winning or losing, only self-realization. He has made and unmade his life several times and now he awaits the golden sunset. There is a hint of melancholy as each day is no longer a dawn of promise. At 100, it cannot be.

As I write this, I have before me, the first American edition of Nirad Babu's masterpiece, *The Autobiography of An Unknown Indian*. Its publication in 1951 made the Unknown Indian known. The book is arguably one of the finest to come out of India this century. On the opening page, Nirad Babu inscribed an Oscar Wilde quotation: 'Anybody can make history. Only a great man can write it.' This was written a few months after our first meeting in late 1954.

I also have with me, *A Passage to England.* Not a masterpiece, but without doubt from the top literary drawer. Here he wrote:

> 'The conversation of the old and young ends generally with contempt or pity on either side', said the great Dr Johnson, but I do not agree, for I have enjoyed Natwar's conversation, and I hope Natwar, too, even though of less than half my age, has enjoyed mine.

This was in July 1959. Nirad Babu was in his sixties, I undeniably, less than half his age.

I have known Nirad C. Chaudhuri most of my adult life. We have had our differences. I am a Forster fan, he, a Kipling admirer. He is severely critical of Gandhi and Nehru. For me they are the great pathfinders of this century. Fortunately our friendship has transcended these disagreements and for me it has been one of the great pleasures of my life.

Nirad Chaudhuri has expanded my literary horizons. He combines in himself the reason of Descartes, the passion of Pascal, the wisdom and serenity of ancient Hindu sages (though outwardly he is noisy and obsessive). In his long life there has never been any spiritual backsliding or intellectual intransigence that led him to abandon the values that made him what he is—the possessor of a granite-like integrity which despises 'saccharine morality'. Not for him the fawning of half-men before authority and power. And if a price had to be paid for this, Nirad C. Chaudhuri has paid it. He owes no debts. He has chosen a hard bed and is content to lie on it. 'Moral discipline was an indispensable preliminary to spiritual achievement', he wrote in his autobiography.

How did we meet? In June 1954 Nirad Babu's attack on E.M. Forster appeared in *Encounter.* I was then at Cambridge and showed it to Forster. He made one or two amusing marginal comments. Nirad C. Chaudhuri had written that Aziz would not have been allowed to enter his house. Forster's reaction was,

'Aziz has elsewhere to go'. That Chaudhuri's assault had gone home, I found out later.

On my return to India, I wrote a short piece on Forster for the *Illustrated Weekly of India* which Nirad Babu read. He referred to it when we met for the first time at a guest night dinner at St. Stephen's College. His first letter to me, dated 17 February 1955 was formal and brief:

> Dear Mr Natawar Singh, (his spelling)
>
> I am sending you a copy of *The Statesman* of 5 February, 1954 in which the article on Deeg appeared. My second son, who wrote it, was nineteen years and four months old at the time. The first son illustrated it with his photographs. We have quite a number of photographs of Deeg, both in colour and black and white. If you are interested you can come and see them on any day convenient to you. You may ring me up at the telephone number given above either before 8.10 a.m. or after 7.30 p.m.
>
> The boy would, however, like to have the article back, as it is one of two copies he has, and usually keeps for file.
>
> It was a great pleasure to meet you, in spite of our different estimates of *A Passage to India.* I am now engaged in a study of Indo-Islamic architecture in the Delhi-Agra region, and hope to do more work on Deeg with your help. The book I want is *Sujan Charitra* by Sudan (*Benaras Nagri Pracharni Sabha*) 2nd edition.
>
> Yours sincerely,
> Nirad C. Chaudhuri

Sujan Charitra is a rare book, which extols the campaigns of Maharaja Suraj Mal of Bharatpur (1707-1763). I secured a copy of the book from Bharatpur and passed it on to Nirad Babu. Thereafter we met several times. To avoid rows we did not mention Forster. I was, therefore, a little surprised when

Nirad Babu on being invited by the British Council and the BBC to visit England in the summer asked me if E.M. Forster would see him. I wrote to Forster. A prompt but typically Forsterian reply made it clear that E.M. Forster had not forgotten the *Encounter* attack. He wrote:

> Now I get your line about Mr Chaudhuri. I had a letter from the British Council earlier, they suggested our meeting and I replied to them that if he cared to write to me direct, I should hope to fix something. It is up to him to write, I think, after the way he snubbed my poor Aziz.

I passed this on to Nirad Babu. The two did meet at Cambridge. Forster was then at the height of his world-wide fame. His books were selling and he was in great demand. Nirad C. Chaudhuri was just beginning to become the not-so-unknown Indian. As far as Forster was concerned, the meeting was pleasant enough. This is how he described the encounter to me:

> I liked Mr Chaudhuri—thought him so at first-hand and it was remarkable how much—and how genuinely he was enjoying English eighteenth century homes, and the pictures of Domenico Veneziano.

In 1959 Nirad Chaudhuri's second book, *A Passage to England* appeared. Forster reviewed it for the *London Observer*. (Nirad Babu told me he would have liked Churchill to review it). Forster's review was generous and fair-minded. Nirad Babu thought it patronizing. Let me quote some portions of the Forster review:

> Besides having integrity and courage, he possesses enthusiasm, cheerfulness and a good English style . . . I have had the pleasure of meeting him once during his visit. His liveliness and intelligence were striking and he made two remarks that particularly impressed me. The first remark was about an unfamiliar Florentine

> painter, Domenico Veneziano. He seemed to know all about Domenico Veneziano and I realized how thorough his cultural preparation for Europe must have been and how much he must have read and reflected.

Forster then came to Aziz—

> The second remark was about my novel, *A Passage to India*. He announced with some firmness that Aziz would never have been admitted into his ancestral home. This does not matter for Aziz, who after all has elsewhere to go, but it made me wonder whether I should have been admitted either.

Forster's review helped sell the book, which he thought 'pleasant and pleasantest when least dogmatic . . .' But Nirad C. Chaudhuri is a dedicated dogmatist. In my review of his book on Clive, I was a bit harsh on him. I wrote that like Macaulay, Nirad C. Chaudhuri had a heightened way of telling things and quoted what Lord Melbourne is reported to have said of Macaulay—'I wish I was as cocksure of anything as Macaulay is of everything.' My conclusion was uncharitable—'for Macaulay, read Chaudhuri'.

In 1961 I left for New York to take up my post in the Permanent Mission of India at the United Nations and Nirad Babu and I lost touch till I saw him again in London seventeen years later. I vividly remember a conversation I had with him before leaving for New York . At the time the question, 'Who after Nehru?', was much discussed. Nirad Chaudhuri's inquiry was provocatively different. For him the question was, 'What, after Nehru?' He told me that after Nehru even the semblance of respectability would disappear. He echoed Churchill's 'men of straw' imperial pessimism. He reminded me of his article entitled 'Personality Cult in Indian Politics' written in 1957. In that article he had written:

> The really dangerous prospect for the country is that there will be no person big enough to be the object of

> the personality cult . . . and after Nehru as things are, nobody will be able to say, as he can with perfect right—*L'etat, c'est moi.* The time has really come for a revivification of personality in Indian politics, and not in denunciation.

I was intrigued by his bias for the cult of personality. Yet, the more I thought about it, the closer I came to agreeing with Nirad Chaudhuri on this point. The Hindus invented the cult of personality. We bestowed divine status on stones. Only a small step was needed to partially transfer that status to a human being. In the twentieth century, the outstanding examples are Gandhi and Nehru. In their case the saving grace was that both were men of distinguished character and possessed a moral aura. Subsequent events showed that the Indian people could just as easily deify lesser mortals.

I followed Nirad Babu's literary career with unfailing interest and some diffidence. In New York, I read *The Continent of Circe* with a sinking feeling and disapproval. It was an angry, even bitter book. It spewed venom at places. The writing was brilliant but the grace of tolerance was missing. His admiration for Kipling went overboard:

> I would also set down, as a matter of moral obligation, that I consider Kipling to be the only English writer who will have a permanent place in English literature with books on Indian themes, and who will also be read by everyone who wants to know not only *British* India but also *timeless* India.

To me this appeared straight out of Baedekar. Timeless India! What in the name of heaven did it mean? I find Kipling's jingoism offensive and offending and I agree with George Orwell, who called Kipling 'morally insensitive and aesthetically disgusting'. And all that tosh about the white man's burden, the Empire, the still upper lip I found nauseating. Worse still Kipling was a racist. In March 1902 he was present at the burial of that inspired imperialist, Cecil Rhodes and read out a specially written poem:

> There, till the vision he foresaw
> Splendid and whole arise.
> And unimagined Empires draw
> To council 'neath his skies,
> The immense and brooding spirit still
> shall quicken and control.
> Living he was the land, and dead,
> His soul shall be her soul.

For almost a century, South African blacks paid with their blood and sweat for the creed and deed of Rhodes. For Nirad C. Chaudhuri, Africa and Africans hardly exist.

In 1970 he settled down in Oxford. In the mid-seventies his biographies of Max Mueller and Robert Clive had been published. Both were well received, but did not add much to his already formidable reputation. We met twice in London and Oxford before I left for Lusaka, Zambia. He was nearing eighty. There was no sign of any depletion of the sources of his creative inspiration. There were, however, hints of his disenchantment with contemporary England, so rapidly in decline. He told me he was working on a book on Hinduism.

I kept in touch with him from the Zambian capital. On 12 January 1978 I received a long letter from him:

> Thank you very much for your letter and for the proof-copy of your piece on me. I found it very interesting and what you have written about E.M. Forster's review of my *Passage* justifies my poor opinion of his character. He aired condescension towards it, which showed what a fool he was. But he was trying to square his account with me.
>
> I follow different principles. I have an article ready pointing out what a poor novel his *Passage* was apart from its shoddy theme. It was full of howlers about Indian life. He made a *Sudra* the brother-in-law of a

> *Brahmin* (both Bengali) and gave the name of Amrit Rao to a Bengali barrister from Calcutta. But I never tried to publish it, because I hold that if I have had personal relations of a satisfactory character with a man, I do not criticize him unless it is a matter of duty.
>
> Even when it is a duty, I do not criticize any one if people might think that I have a personal reason to write unfavourably. The *New York Review of Books* offered me $500 to write of Ved Mehta's book on India. Since he was blind that book could not be authentic. But I told the Editor that since Ved Mehta had spread calumnies (all falsehoods) about me in this book, people might misunderstand me.

He then pulled me up for my review of Ved Mehta's book *Gandhi and His Apostles* which appeared in the *Financial Times*, London. It was not over effusive or too laudatory, but Nirad C. Chaudhuri felt otherwise. His letter goes on to say:

> I cannot understand how you could write favourably about his book on Gandhi. What can a pot-boiler (efficient) writing for an American public (who will never buy a book on India, which is authentic) understand about Gandhi—especially about his sexual obsession. Gandhi's sexuality is not to be understood in terms of the Kinsey Report, or the *Psychapathia Sexualis*. Hindu sexuality is of a brand which is its own. When you read my book on Hinduism, you will get a glimpse of its real character and be startled. Do you want an advance proof copy to read? If so, let me know if I can send it to you through the High Commission here. Though you come from Brij, you do not know what Krishna of Brij is?
>
> You want to know what I think of Amita Malik's piece on me in *The Times of India*. Well, I am certainly flattered, but I also know that what others write about me must be their image of me. I have a

> readymade formula to embody my view of other people's view of me. I am often asked: 'We hear so many stories about you. Are they true? I reply, 'If they are for me, you should discount 95 per cent, but if against, the whole of 100 per cent.'

In the 25 June 1978 issue of the *Illustrated Weekly of India*, he wrote:

> On the whole I should be reconciled to my ill-fame. But a recent comment on me in this paper by my young friend Kunwar Natwar Singhji has given me the idea of delivering a sermon on the subject. He wrote: 'His reputation as an Anglophile is his doing, but he is a better Indian than most of us'. He also observed that I should continue to stir the Indian air so that he and others could breathe freely. This was very handsome of the Kunwar Sahib, and I in my turn would say to him: 'To support me is more patriotic than becoming a champion of E.M. Forster'. Anyway I am obeying his admonition, in order to turn a jet of compressed air over the greasily dirty surface of our cultural life today.

I replied a few weeks later in the same paper that, 'it is better to be a champion of Forster than to be a cheer leader for Kipling.'

I reviewed his book *Hinduism* for the *Financial Times*, when it was published by Chatto and Windus. I liked it but considered it a competent work rather than an inspired one. Nirad C. Chaudhuri did not say much about Buddhism and no study of Hinduism can neglect the Buddha and his teachings. He is not even mentioned in the index. He also, to some extent, exaggerated Greek influence on Hinduism. I pointed out that he was on unsure ground when he asserted that the ancient Persians were 'protected against the temple cult by their exclusive monotheism'. I pointed out that one had only to look up the *Encyclopaedia Brittanica* to discover that the Persians were not 'exclusive monotheists'. I concluded with these words:

> What impact will this beautifully written serious book on so important a subject make in India. Not much, I fear, because in India, that is Bharat, it will fall into that great void where the only echo is oum-boum. The effort was no doubt worth it. As the Gita has it, 'Thou art entitled to the work but never to its fruits.'

While in Zambia, I had finished my biography of Maharaja Suraj Mal (1707-1763). It was published by Allen and Unwin in early 1981. I requested Nirad Babu to review it. He very kindly did. In September he wrote to me at Islamabad:

> I am enclosing the screed on your book. You may use it in any form you like, or get it published as a full length review. I hope you will like it.
>
> I might tell you privately that there are a number of bad misprints in it, and one which is the worst is on p. 34 in the line 'The Jatni did not in vain bear the pain of travel'. English printers have become so illiterate that they do no longer know the word travail.
>
> There is another point to which I would draw your attention. The index has Najib Khan and Najib-ud-Dalah as if they were two different persons.
>
> I might tell you that the picture (traditional portrait) of Suraj Mal which you print was seen by me first when I was a school boy in a text book of history published so far as I remember by Indian Macmillan. That was as far back as 1911 or 1912.
>
> Last of all, I would thank you for giving me a copy of your book. Let me also know what you thought of my latest article in *The Times of India.*

I was very touched by what he wrote about my book. He was eighty-four and it involved him in a labour which he could have done without.

In 1982 I had a long conversation with him at Oxford shortly before his eighty-fifth birthday. He was in excellent form. I asked him if the philosophy of *karma* had any meaning for him: Nirad Babu's response was, 'No, none whatsoever. *Karma* has no meaning. I have no belief in previous birth. I do not believe in future birth. It all ends here. I have talked to you about my religion, my faith. These are based on a fundamental existence of death, of death as a final end of an individual's life. All religions have been based on belief in another world, belief in survival after death. My personal religion is not based on that at all. We end with death. Every individual ends with death. We are parts of universal energy.'

I then asked, if like Thomas Hardy, he believed in chance. He replied: 'Let me explain. It seems chance to me for the simple reason that I have no foreknowledge but it may not be chance. It may be part of a design, who knows. Now, I do believe in Hardy. Hardy is very perverse in this sense. The things that happened to Hardy would never have happened to me. But my case is very curious in this sense—every step seems to be a chance. Why did I not perish by chance instead of surviving by chance. So, my survival seems to be purposive towards some end.

What about sudden fame. Was he surprised on becoming an instant celebrity? 'No', he replied, fame did not come suddenly. 'I thought I would get it when my autobiography appeared. I expected recognition. So, in a way I was not surprised. Certain things pleased me very much. I, somehow, very foolishly lost faith in the immortality of the soul, retained faith in the immortality of the mind as perpetuated in my books. Only writers can be assured immortality for themselves. Not princes. Only a writer gets that kind of immortality. Nobody else.'

After the publication of *Hinduism* he started work on volume two of his autobiography. He completed the book by 1986.

It is not widely known that Nirad Babu had considerable difficulty in placing *Thy Hand, Great Anarch*! with a publisher. The book was nearly a thousand pages long. When he sent the manuscript to Chatto and Windus they threw up their hands. Who would read a book of such length? They asked Nirad Babu to reduce it to 350 pages. The author's response was characteristically unambiguous. Not a page would be withdrawn. Take it or leave it. That was that. The book was not to be published.

When I got to know this from mutual friends, I was distressed and not a little annoyed. What a way to treat an author of Nirad C. Chaudhuri's calibre. The man was almost a living literary shrine. Then chance intervened. Early in 1987, a delegation of leading British publishers arrived in Delhi. With them came Graham Greene, a senior director of Chatto and a nephew of the novelist. I spoke to him about Chatto's shabby treatment of India's outstanding man of letters. The least Chatto could do was to give Nirad C. Chaudhuri a ninetieth birthday present by publishing the book. Graham Greene, whom I was meeting for the first time, knew nothing about the Chaudhuri book. On returning to London he reversed the earlier decision. *Thy Hand* appeared in late 1987, without any cuts and was well received by critics and readers. Nirad C. Chaudhuri got to know of my intervention and thanked me. We, however, agreed not to make this public till now.

Thy Hand revived interest in Nirad Babu and three years later Oxford University bestowed a Doctorate on him. I played a minor, unpublicized role here too.

In June 1988, I was one of the speakers at the opening session of the twenty-third International Publishers Association Congress in London. Lord Jenkins, Wole Soyinka, UNESCO Director-General Frederico Mayor and Mrs Hosni Mubarak were the other speakers. At lunch I sat next to Roy Jenkins, who was Chancellor of Oxford University. I spoke to him at some length about Nirad C. Chaudhuri. He was familiar with the name, but had not realized that the writer lived in Oxford. I suggested that should be given some recognition by Oxford. Jenkins took out his notebook and scribbled something. He made no commitment and rightly so.

Less than two years later it happened.

On 3 March 1990, Nirad C. Chaudhuri was presented the Honorary Degree of Doctor of Letters by the Oxford University. The speech by the Public Orator was delivered in Latin:

> The eminent Bengali whom I now present is thoroughly versed both in English and European poetry and has interpreted Indian society and customs to us with great intellectual ability, illuminating incidentally several aspects of our own society . . . . Mr Chaudhuri expressed his views on contemporary events with a frankness which was too great to make him popular with his fellow Indians, praising certain aspects of the Raj, and lacking in the requisite enthusiasm for the birth of New India. But with the passage of time his reputation at home is now restored. The Unknown Indian of his book has deservedly won fame and recognition.

It has been a long journey from Kishorganj of the 1890s to the Oxford of the 1990s. When I met him some months later he told me how much the degree meant to him.

I can think of no other writer in history who was still writing at the age of 100. Nirad Chaudhuri is not only an intellectual inferno, he is also a scholarly tsar. His latest book is about the decline of human civilization. It is not 'a rehash of Spengler but a sequel to him'. He is pained by the decline he sees in England—'They seem to take pride in decrying their imperial greatness'. His is a disturbing view of Indian society. Those who elect to swim against the current invite the wrath of the world. His outlook has not changed for the past seventy-five years. In 1947 he had written:

> All that we have learnt, all that we have acquired, and all that we have prized is threatened with extinction. We do not know how this end will come, whether through a cataclysmic holocaust or slow putrid decay. But regarding the eventual extinction there does not seem to be any uncertainty.

These are hard and worrying words. It is totally defeatist and a surrender to despair. I do not wholly share Nirad C. Chaudhuri's dark vision, but I do accept it as a warning. Here is a man who has thought deeply on life's vagaries and whims. His judgements cannot be simply brushed aside. In his book on Max Mueller, he wrote:

> Last of all, the life of Max Mueller as lived by him faces us with an absolutely fundamental question, to which I shall certainly try to give an answer. It is this: Is the life of a scholar—thinker worth living? It is no use dismissing this question by taking for granted the scholar's role in a civilized society. Most of our incomprehension of life comes from not facing upto this sort of question; for disregarding Plato's profound maxim that the unexamined life—*anexatastos bios*—is not worth living.

As our pre-eminent scholar-thinker, Nirad Babu has touched 'on universal and timeless interests' and the grandeur of his intellectual life has been a beacon of light for us all. At the same time I keep hoping that Nirad C. Chaudhuri will turn out to be a false prophet.

THE WOUNDED CONTINENT, AND NIRAD BABU AND NAIPAUL

Keki N. Daruwalla

To take up a book like *The Continent of Circe* for a centennial salute to an author as celebrated as Nirad C. Chaudhuri, would seem to some a deliberate exercise in perversity. (All perversity is deliberate, incidentally). For after all, *Circe*, (pronounced Kirké, according to my father's Classical Dictionary[1]) is the sorceress who turned people into swine[2]. The book, for all its historical sweep and its cornucopia of insights, is in its essence, an essay on environmental fatalism, a lament on the fate of the Aryan who left his homeland in Europe only to be caught and left squeezed-out and enervated in the steamy heat of the Indo-Gangetic plain. While it may be rash to hazard an opinion on how posterity will treat him, as scholar, biographer, historian or a man of ideas, scholarship (*Clive of India, Scholar Extraordinary: Life of F. Max Mueller*) may not perhaps earn him the encomiums he may consider due to him. *Thy Hand, Great Anarch! India 1921-52* may be a massively informative tome (979 pages), but its mixture of autobiography and history leaves one uneasy. Even that wonderfully evocative *Autobiography of an Unknown Indian* is already fading from public memory. But it is his polemical writing with which Nirad Chaudhuri will be identified, and no better example of it can be found than *The Continent of Circe*[3].

As a sounding board and parallel text I could think of nothing more apt than V.S. Naipaul's *India: A Wounded Civilization.*[4] *An Area of Darkness* was his first book on India, and has been heavily trampled upon by liverish Indian critics and xenophobes. Though written during the Emergency clamped by Mrs Gandhi on an unsuspecting nation, *A Wounded Civilization* is not totally coloured by this one event. It is reflective of Mr Naipaul's general views on India.

Diasporas play a big part in the philosophic make up of both writers. Nirad Chaudhuri is obsessed with the Aryan drift into tropical India. For the Aryan settler the axis of history turned (for the worse), once, to borrow from Iqbal's phraseology, the Aryan caravan unsaddled itself on the banks of the Ganga. For Naipaul it is the shift of indentured labour from Bihar and U.P. to the Caribbean which is the starting point of his emotional involvement with India. The event is dredged out in his unceasing Indian odyssey, as he keeps at it like a lost root tugging away at a forgotten nerve of racial memory.

Both put the Indian past under a microscope. Both view the present skeptically. Nirad Babu is vociferous and stentorian in his condemnation, his writing bristling with moral and intellectual outrage. Naipaul's perspectives mellow only later in the Nineties with his *India: A Million Mutinies Now.* But there is an air of brooding pessimism in all that he has to say about India in his earlier book. Both writers try and hide their affection for the country, Chaudhuri under the stern facade of an angry elder, Naipaul behind the surgeon's mask, a surgeon still examining his patient on the operating table.

Nirad Chaudhuri has a conceptual framework carefully worked out, perhaps over half a lifetime. Naipaul moves from hotel room to hotel room, his suitcase full of insights and an occasional banality. Chaudhuri is rooted in the land, its landscape, its culture its mother language, Sanskrit, its scriptures. Naipaul is the perennial itinerant, returning like a seabird to the site of an old shipwreck.

Naipaul is sensitive to the point of squeamishness when it comes to squalor and stink. Chaudhuri at least pretends to be unconcerned. He doesn't regard a man 'a fit citizen of India' until he becomes 'indifferent to the presence of fifty lepers in various stages of decomposition within a hundred yards and the sight of ubiquitous human excreta everywhere.'

Naipaul is like a mother bird rummaging in a nest of doubts. Nirad is blessed with certitudes that almost reek of arrogance.

Nirad Chaudhuri's is a predatory bird's eye view of the entire Aryan existence in the Indo-Gangetic plain, a final verdict (all his verdicts are final) on Hindu character as it has evolved during three millennia and how the climate has debased him. 'To put the matter briefly, the Hindu is the European distorted, corrupted and made degenerate by the cruel torrid environment and by the hostility, both real and imagined, of the true sons of the soil.' His is an enquiry into the origins of Indian philosophy, a philosophy of sorrow prompted by the motive to rescue the world from sorrow. He hammers home the point that the intellectual motivation to the development of a body of thought is missing. 'The Hindu never represented human suffering as anything but the ills flesh is heir to. Even Hindu salvation, which is release from sorrow, is reduced to terms of the flesh.' And again when he says, 'The philosophies did not make our life what it is, it was the life which made the philosophies what they are.'

But along with such splendid insights you also get a load of dismissive dogma. If Circe turned men into swine, Nirad Chaudhuri can reduce complex philosophies into trite simplifications. Buddhism gets condensed and dismissed (if not vilified) in exactly four lines: Siddhartha 'decided to leave the world' because of three epiphanies in reverse, his chance encounters with a cadaverous old man, the sick and the dead. Chaudhuri now takes off. 'Can anyone conceive of a more pitiful failure, from the moral point of view, of courage, and from the biological of vitality? Where would a man stand in regard to faith and effort once he allowed himself to be intimidated by the commonplace lot of all flesh?'[5]

Chaudhuri's India, walled in by the Himalayas, is a sort of a hothouse where only a certain kind of people can thrive; a people thoroughly self-conscious of their identity, bloodkins operating through caste, a people who considered themselves not a Chosen People but *The People*; a people who believed that their 'way of life is divinely ordained and eternal; that I was superior to all others; that there was an unbridgeable gulf between them and the older inhabitants of the country, as well as foreigners.'[6] Needless to say these people are Hindus. He does not take cognizance of others. There is a racial (?) exclusivity about his definition of an Indian. When foreigners speak of 'an Indian' he tells them: 'Please do not use that word (Indian). Say "Hindu" if you have in mind a human type common to the whole continent; otherwise if you have a group in mind say Bengali, Punjabi, Hindustani, Marathi, Tamil, Sikh, Muslim.' The religious minorities have been reduced to provincial status and denied an All India character. And what does he mean by Hindustani? That's the Hindi word for an Indian, isn't it? Perhaps for a Bengali like him, it would mean a North Indian.

I have related the above at length because when I was at Oxford for a year and was seated next to him at a party he kept referring to Ayatollah Khomeini as 'your Khomeini.' When I reminded him that Parsis had been living in India for over thirteen hundred years, he said: 'You don't become an Indian in thirteen hundred years.'

Most historians hedge their bets when it comes to details about the Aryan advance into India. Not so Chaudhuri who speaks emphatically, even as he traverses the quicksands of historic speculation that this era is rife with. 'Whatever the date, it was the confrontation of the Aryans, the first civilized people to settle in India proper, with the dark primitives that set in motion the continuous ethnic history of India.'[7] He has no place for the very civilized Indus Valley people, it seems. When the Aryans arrived they found that 'all the Darks of the country had virtually become fused into one mass'. Can such statements go unchallenged? Even today we see a plethora of tribes, each with its distinctive culture, customs and dialect. And he keeps talking of the encounter between 'a fair-complexioned civilized people, and the dark-skinned and, to them, savage people.' The colour bit is rammed down repeatedly, though he is of course right when he talks of the original settlers as hunters (dark always) and the Aryans as pastoral and agriculturists, and lest we forget, fair.

North-west India Nirad Babu hands over to the 'Middle Eastern Zone', much in the manner of Zulfiqar Ali Bhutto who after the 1971 defeat and the breaking away of its eastern wing, kept saying that Pakistan was now a part of West Asia rather than South Asia. The Aryan migration from Persia to India he ascribes to the rise of an intolerant monotheism in Persia. This would make the migration a post-Zarathushtra phenomenon because earlier the water goddess Anahita, mythologically derived from Ishtar, was placed almost on the same pedestal as Ahura Mazda. People like Annie Besant placed Zoroaster somewhere around 10,000 B.C.! Later writers made him a contemporary of Buddha and Mahavira. (Karl Jaspers may have had this in mind when he talked of the 'axial years' ranging from 800 to 200 B.C.—years that changed the course of human civilization.) Now increasingly Zarathushtra is being slotted between 1500 and 1200 B.C. Would the Aryan migration be as recent as that?

The migration is fairly central to Chaudhuri's thesis. For the Aryan paradise was lost when they left Iran. The *Devas* were defeated and the *Asuras* won. And while in Indian myth the gods recover their heaven, 'but in history paradise is lost for ever.'[8]

But when we leave the Aryans behind, tramping through some of the arid acres of Chaudhuri's arguments can be a bit trying. For instance, the pages on Hindu capital and Hindu socialism superimposing the *varna* factor on the Private versus Public Sector debate; the industrialization of the *Adivasi* regions which he opposes, an argument he caps with a slightly pseudo poetic and hyperbolic flight of fancy. The glare from the Tata

Steel furnaces at Jamshedpur seems, to Chaudhuri, 'to rise from the gigantic and unquenchable funeral pyre of the primitives.' There is also that bit about the chemical action of the secular state on the *Bania*, resulting in the unleashing of even greater avarice than before and making him 'even more evil than Milton's fallen angel.' Such poeticisms can let him down on occasion. Yet he can sometimes redeem a sterile argument with a twist in the end, which one can only ascribe to inspiration. 'The old Aryan did indeed degrade them (the tribals) on the plains, but he spared them in the wilds. The industrialized Hindu State will carry the servitude and degradation to the home territory of the aboriginals.' You may quarrel with the logic but the passage has all the aplomb of a heroic couplet from Alexander Pope.

Uncharacteristically, one gets the impression that Chaudhuri's treatment of the caste system is an exercise in apologetics. There is, of course, much to be said for the caste system as federation. But one gets the feeling that he is unnecessarily trying to elevate the *Sudra*. Just because the tribals were even worse off does not elevate the *Sudra*. 'The servile Darks were untouchable; the *Sudras* though theoretically servile in function, were not so: they were part of the Hindu society, not outside it.' *Sudras* only 'theoretically servile'? Really, Chaudhuri! To strengthen his argument, as a member of the *Kayastha* community he numbers himself among the *Sudras*, technically. The *Kayasthas* formed the bureaucratic core of the Mughal court—scribe, keeper of land records, financial advisor and men of letters, when such men were scarce. Raja Todarmal who framed and implemented the Moghul revenue policy and was numbered among the 'nine jewels' (*nau ratna*) of the court, was a *Kayastha*. They formed the elite.

Considerable emphasis has been laid on the Central Asian hordes being despised as *Mlechcha* because they came as conquerors and hurt Indian pride. But let us not forget that the *desi Sudra* was similarly branded.

One is grateful to Chaudhuri that he has discussed at length the 'incorrigible militarism of the Hindus' through the ages. It is good to know that Ayodhya was no atavistic throwback to some primordial state of savagery. It was a part of good old Hindu tradition. Could one wish Bal Thackeray a successful *ashvamedh*? Nirad Babu says: 'Though Maurya imperialism was certainly imitative of Cyrus the Achaemenian, the kings of the dynasty did not imitate the humanity of Cyrus. Their methods of war were Assyrian, and recall in their killings and deportations the ferocity of an *Ashur-nasir-pal*.' He also advances the rather bold thesis that in the twenty-three centuries between Ashoka and Gandhi 'there is not *one word* of non-violence in the theory and practice of statecraft by the Hindus.'

While enumerating Hindu follies, he himself falls a prey to the Hindu way of thinking and articulation. (Could it possibly have been any different?) 'Most Hindu rebels, amongst whom I would also include the Sikhs, claimed with justice that they were fighting for *Dharma*.' The Hindu embrace is one thing the Sikh wants to disentangle himself from. And the more he wishes to establish his separate identity the more assertively the Hindu reminds him of his Hindu heritage, and that he is just a militant Hindu. The early twentieth-century pamphlet brought out by the Sikhs and published in 1901 or 1902, was significantly titled *Hum Hindu Nahin Hain* (We are Not Hindus).

A chapter on Muslims, entitled, 'The Least of the Minorities' is almost a straightforward account of the political history of the Muslims this century. Islam, the orientation given to it in India, the theological divides between the Muslim schools of thought are not Chaudhuri's strong suit. The Khilafat movement, the Hindu-Muslim unity during the Non-Cooperation movement in 1920-22 and the falling apart during the Civil Disobedience movement of 1930-32 are touched upon. Always one to call a spade a spade, he brings out the Anglo-Muslim liaison. Ironically, generations have been brought up in Pakistan on the theory of an Anglo-Hindu hook-up! He has some rough things to say about the Partition.[9] But he is clearly off the mark when he suggests that the first plank of Indian foreign policy was to isolate Pakistan from her natural friends. By this, one supposes, he means the Middle East. By joining the Anglo-American capitalist block Pakistan could expect little sympathy from the Nasserites who had caught the imagination of the Arab world. Pakistan kept quiet when the Suez crisis occurred. One of its Prime Ministers made a famous statement as to why he was not close to Arab countries: 'Because zero plus zero plus zero is, after all and only, equal to zero.' And Pakistan lectured established Islamic countries on Islam. King Farouq of Egypt got so irritated that he once remarked that he knew that Islam was born on 14 August 1947! Pakistan didn't need any adversaries to isolate it.

But it is the chapter entitled 'The Half-Caste Minorities: Genetic and Cultural' where the title makes his intentions clear. One need not pay much heed to his disclaimer that 'It is with utmost reluctance that I write this chapter.' To quote the wolf in my rather irreverent sally into verse:

> He said 'I am loath, I really am
> to eat you up my dear lamb.
> But can I help if cussed fate
> puts you on my dinner plate?'

He articulates the most stereotypical racial prejudices and dredges out the worst quotations on 'miscegenation' from Bhishma to Kipling.[10] Discussing the uninhibited ways of the Eurasian and Goanese Liliths (his words, not mine) he blames the Hindus for the 'cowardly assault on the reputation and morals of weak communities which cannot resist the money, power and lust of the dominant order.' There is the other side of course. 'By making sensuality easier to satisfy and more piquant in the satisfaction, the two communities (Eurasians and Goans) show themselves as the seducers of the Hindus.'

But Nirad Babu is never afraid of saying what he wants to. Discussing the antithetical traits of the Hindus, he lists them accordingly: 'A sense of Hindu solidarity with an uncontrollable tendency towards disunity within the Hindu order; collective megalomania with self-abasement; extreme xenophobia with abject xenolatry; authoritarianism with anarchic individualism; violence with non-violence; militarism with pacifism; possessiveness with carelessness about property owned; courage with cowardice;

cleverness with stupidity.' When someone can be that egalitarian in his denunciations, how can he ever be accused of partiality?

'Damnation, one may imagine, is an easier subject than salvation to handle artistically,' said Maurice Cranston in an essay on Sartre. That observation would hold good both for Nirad Chaudhuri and V.S. Naipaul. A damp melancholia settles on Naipaul whenever he visits India, or even when he thinks of it. Some of us had no idea we could be that depressing. His writings on India are travelogues in both senses. He is of course travelling physically. Metaphorically, he is travelling through India's history, art, myth. But it is surface contact. Depth needs time, roots. Yet his mind is so rapier-sharp that the insights he gleans from this contact are valuable and every bit worth the reader's while.

Naipaul manages to come here at the worst of times. For his *An Area of Darkness* he had to come in 1962. For *India: A Wounded Civilization* it was the magnet of the Emergency that drew him in. Who knows, Laloo Yadav's antics may drag him here again? His visits are not easy. 'India is for me a difficult country. It isn't my home and cannot be my home; and yet I cannot reject it or be indifferent to it; I cannot travel only for the sights. I am at once too close and too far.'

India's narcissistic self-obsession is known. Muhammad Bin Qasim's invasion caught us unprepared. 'No civilization was so little equipped to cope with the outside world; no country was so easily raided and plundered and learned so little from its disasters.' The India of 1947 'was a land of far older defeat.' Vijayanagar, that 'long-superseded civilization' gives him the right setting for expounding on defeat. Muslim ruin heaped on Hindu ruin makes him wonder about India's thousand-year-old intellectual retreat before its conquerors; and whether in its apparent revivals 'India hadn't been making itself archaic again.'

In effect *A Wounded Civilization* propounds the theory, if that is what it can be called, of the inability of the Indian to come to terms with the outside world, its outlook and values or with the squalor, inequity and the cruelty of his own surroundings.[11] 'The world outside India was to be judged by its own standards. India was not to be judged. India was only to be experienced in the Indian way.' The security the Indian craves for he finds in his caste identity or in following the dictates of his personal *guru*, as Jagan follows Gandhi in Narayan's novel, *The Vendor of Sweets*. After freedom is won, Jagan is fair to his customers and only cheats the government of the country for which he got beaten by the police then. Since Gandhi never told him to pay his sales tax, he didn't pay it. That, of course, is Narayan's private joke but Naipaul gets a foothold here to build on his argument regarding Indian ethics.

Jagan's son returns from America with a half-Korean half-American wife to set up, with US collaboration, a plant that will manufacture a story-writing machine. I am glad that Naipaul finds 'the satire too gross, the newcomers too outlandish.' People like R.K. Narayan get apotheosized so quickly in our country that criticism becomes sacrilege. Jagan's subsequent behaviour, barricading himself against the couple, selling his sweets cheaply and reading the Gita to his staff, Naipaul ascribes to 'the intrusion of alien elements.' Jagan becomes a metaphor, a paradigm of typical Indian behaviour. 'To be pure in the midst of "the grime of this earth", secure in the midst of distress: that is all he asks. When his world shatters, he cannot fight back; he has nothing to offer. Another Hindu retreat—like the Vijayanagar kingdom in 1336, like the pilgrims worshipping among the ruins of Vijayanagar in 1975, like the *mantra* being chanted and written fifty million times to give life to the image of the temple defiled during the war.' Naipaul tends to get carried away.

And yet Narayan's gentle world baffles him, for this is not the India Naipaul has gleaned from newspapers or his interviews with slum dwellers and villagers in the typical manner of the foreign correspondent. So he finds Vijay Tendulkar's world crueller and closer to the ground. But the gentler Indian reality, far removed from mayhem, oppression and social chaos, which R.K. Narayan portrays is unknown to him.

One of the strengths of this book is that Naipaul dissects quite a few literary texts to arrive at the heart of his Indian darkness. Starting with R.K. Narayan's *Mr Sampath*, and *The Vendor of Sweets* he goes on to Ananthamurti's *Samskar* and later to Vijay

Tendulkar's plays. This is a refreshing change from Nirad Chaudhuri who only leans back on Kipling in *The Continent of Circe.* In some other books of his he refers to Bengali writers. *Desi* writers in English are, of course, beneath Nirad Babu's notice, though Khushwant Singh does get a not exactly honourable mention in the preface.

At times Naipaul seems to be going around with almost a notebook in hand, recording his impressions rather feverishly. There are long sterile passages in the book where he tells us about visits with the Commissioner to some village in Bundi or meeting some silly woman or journalist at a dinner. What is more, he chooses to quote their inanities. This can become a bit wearing. And, when he is caught off guard, he gives the impression of looking down. Take this passage: 'A rich man indeed, this Patel, to have his own well! . . . And the Patel had something else no one in the village had: an outhouse, a latrine!' Such sneering belittles the earlier Naipaul. One does not find this in his *India: A Million Mutinies Now.*

Actually *A Wounded Civilization* is an essay on the Indian defeat—in thought, action, past and present history. Defeat is not something that came with the fall of Vijayanagar (symbolic isn't it, the fall of the 'City of Victory'?) or 1962 or the failure of democracy, brazenly demonstrated by the Emergency. Naipaul's interest lies in mapping out the contours of defeat on the landscape of the Indian mind. Withdrawal and opting out are the important signposts here—from the outer squalor to a degree of inner purity (never achieved), from social turmoil to some sort of personal equanimity, however elusive. And implicit in the argument is the absence of a social contract within Indian society, tradition or the state. Take this little nugget on the mass conversion of *Harijans* to Buddhism after 1947: 'The assertion of pride, a contracting out, a regrouping: it is the pattern of such movements among the dispossessed or humiliated.'

And he doesn't see a synthesizing role for modern Indian as between the East and the West, the modern and the traditional. No such grandiose (and myopic) Tagorean vision for him. We specialize not in ideas but obsessions. 'Indians say their gift is for synthesis. It might be said, rather, that for far too long, as a conquered people, they have been intellectually parasitic on other civilizations. To survive in subjection, they have preserved their sanctuary of the instinctive, uncreative life, converting that into a religious ideal; at a more worldly level, they have depended on others for the ideas and institutions that make a country work.'[12]

Naipaul is painstaking and tries to see the working of the xenophobic Shiv Sena on the ground. He finds a lot of improvements the Sena has brought about in squatter's colonies and chawls, though he does mention 'the theatricality of its leader, a failed cartoonist who is said to admire Hitler.' But he can be easily misled. Because he saw a portrait of Ambedkar during his tour of the *chawls*, he thinks the Sena is pro-*Harijan* and 'very different from the Sena the newspapers wrote about.' Vijay Tendulkar tells him that there is a connection between the Naxalites and the Kali cult and her skull necklaces, and he believes it!

One of his most perceptive chapters is on Gandhi, entitled 'A Defect of Vision'. He points out that in *My Experiments with Truth*, his famous biography, Gandhi is so terribly self-absorbed that he notices nothing of England, which he is visiting for the first time. There is nothing about the voyage barring the fact that he did not know the use of knife and fork, and so took his food, mostly sweets and fruit, in the cabin. Not a word about the ports that the ship must have touched. Despite three years in England there is not a word about the climate or the seasons, or of the London of 1890, the capital of the world. He meets Edwin Arnold, who becomes the vice president of the vegetarian club which Gandhi ran at Bayswater. But not a mention of his poetry or a conversation with him. The only 'authors' or 'editors' mentioned are of a book *The Ethics of Diet* or the magazine *The Vegetarian*! Was he so obsessed with his dietary fads? I've known people here, the no-garlic no-onion types, who ate bread only made out of a flour of dried water nuts *(singhara)* or buck-wheat and hence fully support Naipaul's thesis. How is it that tomes have been written on Gandhi and yet no one has pointed these things out.

In South Africa, Gandhi does not mention the Africans enough, thinks Naipaul. All that the atrocities on them impel Gandhi to do is to take a vow of celibacy at the age of thirty-seven.[12] But, says Naipaul, and this is crucial, 'Landscape is never described.' He says in the entire book there are only three gratuitous references to landscape. How typically Indian! (Editing a book on Indian poetry in English this writer found that apart from a poet or two, not a single one noticed the landscape. They were all obsessed with their inner this or inner that, and not a line on bird or vegetation or mountain.)

The admiration for Gandhiji, of course, comes through and Naipaul finds him magnificent in Noakhali. But in Vinoba Bhave, whom he calls a parody of Gandhi, he finds, nothing redeeming. Perhaps Bhave's muted support of the Emergency coloured Naipaul's views further.

Apart from Sudhir Kakar there is just one Indian Mr Naipaul quotes with approval—Nirad Chaudhuri, who else? Both Naipaul and Nirad Chaudhuri bring a laser-like quality to their probing of the Indian condition. Naipaul gets upset and baffled by the reality here, and the Indian response to defeat—the recourse not just to ritual and *mantra*, but to the fatalism of the past.

Today this same escape route takes the shape of a nostalgia for the Gandhian paradise of oxen and plough and the spinning wheel, the past chanted like a spell—*swarajya*, *Ramrajya*— thus offering the 'solace of incantation.'

It is abstractions that bother Nirad Babu. If the absolute, or the universal *atma* lacks a definition, he is not happy. 'A very large part of what is called Hindu-thinking is wooly speculation or mush.' But unlike Naipaul, he does not think that Hindu metaphysics served as a sanctuary for escapists. 'Our metaphysical systems were not erected for their own sake, but for a practical end,' he says. Both talk of the failure of Hindu thought. 'But once it is admitted that Hindu philosophy is a philosophy of failure on a bodily plane, it must also be acknowledged that it has given to that failure a grandeur of expression which no mere failure could ever hope to have.' Chaudhuri sounds heroic even while discussing failure. Naipaul, less versed in, and hence less cognizant of the immense reach of Hindu philosophy, gets depressed. The worm of doubt is a significant presence with both writers. One can only contrast this with the stubborn defiance of someone like Mohammad Iqbal who said that Islam had never failed the Muslim. Whenever they had faced defeat and discomfiture, it was because Muslims had failed Islam.

Both Nirad Chaudhuri and V.S. Naipaul, each in his own way, and using different weapons, one a bludgeon and the other a rapier, have probed the vulnerabilities of the Indian reality. V.S. Naipaul has modified his views a bit. Nirad Chaudhuri is not likely to change. One can quarrel with his opinions and some of his obvious prejudices which leave a sour taste in the mouth. (One should never be appalled at what he says, because that is precisely the response he is trying to elicit). But one can't deny the originality of the views, the quality of his quicksilver mind and the passion and the integrity behind his sweeping denunciations.

Chapter Notes

1. *A Dictionary of Classical Antiquities: Mythology, Religion, Literature and Art* from the German Dr Oskar Seyfert. Revised and edited by Henry Nettleship and J.E. Sandys, London, William Glashier Ltd, 1894.
2. Circe (Kirké). A celebrated magician, daughter of the Sun (Helios) and the Ocean nymph Perseis, sister of Aetes and Pasiphae. She dwelt on the island of Aeae.
   (She turns a part of Odysseus' crew to swine, but with the help of Hermes he compels her to restore them to their human shape, and spends a whole year with her in pleasure and enjoyment and begets a son by her, Telegonus).
3. Publ. Chatto & Windus, London, 1965.
4. Publ. Andre Deutsch, 1977.
5. *The Continent of Circe* (p. 145).
6. ibid. p. 35.
7. ibid. p. 45.
8. ibid. p. 50.

9. ibid. p. 243.

'Yet within six months it (the Partition) was announced as a policy, and accepted as a proposal, and in less than three months from the announcement of the plan the monstrous and unnatural partition of India became a fact. The Hindus and the British alike foreswore the principle of unity of India which they had always professed. This was made possible by a combination of three factors—Hindu stupidity in the first instance and Hindu cowardice afterwards, British opportunism, and Muslim fanaticism.'

10. ibid. p. 258-259.

'In the Mahabharata, Yudisthira asks Bhishma, 'Grandfather! How can we recognize a half-caste who is born of the seed of a man of inferior caste in the womb of a woman of superior caste, but who looks or dresses like an Arya?' Bhishma replies, 'The baseness of a man born of miscegenation is easily detected from his un-Aryan conduct; indiscriminate habits, cruelty, non-observance of rituals proclaim the low origin of these men; . . . they can never hide their baseness; just as tigers and other animals cannot give up their nature, these men too cannot . . . mere knowledge of the sacred books cannot remove the baseness of a base man. So it goes on.'

'Not all! their eyes are blued and their nails are blackened with low-caste blood, many of them. Sons of *mehteranees*—brothers-in-law to the *bhungi* (sweeper)'.

11. India: *A Wounded Civilization.* p. 32.
12. ibid. p. 134
13. ibid. p. 100
14. ibid. p. 138-139

'I come upon people, both men and women, who seem to enjoy being ill-treated by others. It is an emotional luxury for them to dwell on and speak about their grievances and wallow in self-pity. Among such people conversation means relating what they suffer at the hands of official superiors or inferiors, relatives near or distant.' This is what the 79-year-old Bengali writer Nirad Chaudhuri wrote in 1970, in *To Live*

> *or Not to Live*, a handbook for Indians on 'living happily with others'. Chaudhuri, beating his own way out of the thicket of Indian attitudes, believes that Indians do not live, that they live 'unsoundly', to no purpose. 'Do we live at all? This would seem an absurd question, for none of us commit suicide, though, to the honest, I would confess that I have come to feel that a large majority of the persons I know should do so, because I cannot see any point in their remaining alive.'

(This reminds me of Voltaire who was going through the writings of a hack. Voltaire was not impressed and asked him why he was writing such stuff. The journalist replied 'one must live'. Pat came the withering answer 'I do not see the necessity').

THE LAST BENGALI BABU

Harish Trivedi

Finding myself in Oxford in the second week of July 1997, I decided on an impulse to phone Nirad Chaudhuri. (I had never been moved to do so on any of my previous visits to Oxford but this, I told myself, was in the cause of HarperCollins!) He himself answered, in a voice light and high-pitched but surprisingly brisk and young. I said I wished to congratulate him on being 100, and he laughed and said that would be premature. 'I don't know whether I'll live on till then,' he said, still laughing; 'one doesn't know about death.' After a moment's pause, he added, gravely, 'Life is suffering.' I said he sounded like a traditional Hindu, and he laughed again and said, 'Yes, yes, I am a Hindu—and I am an Englishman!' He seemed to be quite pleased with himself uttering this paradoxical, would-be shocking formulation of his identity, and when I laughed at it, he too laughed some more, in a genial, giggly kind of way, at his rhetorical trick having worked. I asked him if I could come and see him briefly, and he asked for my name again. A long silence followed, and then he asked for my name yet again. I could almost hear the wheels whirring of his mental RAM; I was obviously not a Bengali, nor was I apparently someone whom anyone had mentioned to him. At last he said, politely and softly, 'I am sorry but I am very feeble and half-blind. My wife died some time ago, and I do not now receive people.' I noticed and liked that 'receive'! The kind of fastidiously cultivated person that he is, he could not of a course simply *meet* people.

I asked him what he had been reading and writing lately, and he instantly brightened again. He had written a book in his hundredth year which was about to come out, he said, again with that gurgling laughter of his. What was it called, I asked him, and he chuckled and said: 'I can't tell you!' 'But how will I look for it then,' I asked, laughing myself, and he laughed back and said, 'Just ask for Mr Chaudhuri's new book!' If this was vanity, it was quite innocent and disarming, and he laughed some more and so did I.

I

Nothing that Nirad Chaudhuri has written in his whole career has been as shocking and as quotable as the very first page of his first book, cheekily titled *The Autobiography of an Unknown India* (1951). This was the very dedication of the book:

> To the memory of the British Empire in India, which conferred subjecthood on us but withheld citizenship; to which yet every one of us threw out the challenge: *Civis Britannicus Sum*, because all that was good and living within us was made, shaped and quickened by the same British rule.

This is 'dedication' in both senses of the term, and indeed

Chaudhuri's whole manifesto. But four years after the Raj had ended, he is already moved by its 'memory' and hankering after it. The British 'conferred' subjecthood on Indians, he says, as if such subjecthood was some special honour or distinction; his regret is that they did not do a thorough enough job and carry the process a stage further. His own definitely minority, if not utterly eccentric, opinion on this matter is then grandly inflated to become the view of 'everyone of us', and then comes the even grander Latin, serving to hector and browbeat the common reader in India to whom it would be inaccessible. And finally, in a nicely structured climax, comes the keynote of Chaudhuri's lifelong belief that it was the British who brought into being (or 'quickened'—in the erudite and arcane Biblical-Shakespearian sense of 'gave or restored life to') *all that was good and living within us* and never mind the tautology. Well, Indian writers in English have always been relatively soft on the Raj but, for the most blatant expression of what has come be called the colonial cringe, this dedication takes the cake.

For all its outrageous imperialist orientation, the *Autobiography* remains one of the minor classics of Indian writing in English, comparable within the genre perhaps only to Nehru's autobiography, with which it rubs shoulders in the BA and MA syllabi of numerous Indian and some foreign universities. It is engagingly (if also ostentatiously) written, it is constantly lively and witty, it is at over 500-pages vast in scope, and its dominant note is not merely narrative but equally discursive and reflective. It is, of course, not so much a biography as it is history and sociology, or, in Chaudhuri's own favourite formulation, 'descriptive ethnology'. In it Chaudhuri acutely observed and imaginatively evoked a cultural world which was somewhat odd and peculiar even when it existed and had quite disappeared by the time he came to recall it.

The scale of the rich and varied social background against which Chaudhuri sets his own individual life is indicated by the fact that he cannot even find the time or the opportunity to get born until he has reached page 132—thus reminding one of the similarly delayed birth of the ever digressive fictional hero Tristram

Shandy. It's only after the social and intellectual stage has been fully and properly set, through a long chapter each on the four given co-ordinates of his life—'My Birthplace,' 'My Ancestral Village', 'My Mother's Village' and 'England'—that Chaudhuri himself can slip into this fascinating world edgeways, as it were. (Incidentally, Chaudhuri's juxtaposition of distant England right beside his mother's village reminds one of his friend Khushwant Singh's boast that his mother tongue is English though his mother knows not a word of it.)

The *mofussil* East Bengal town of Kishorganj, where Chaudhuri was born, has been described so fully and fondly by him that it has become a celebrated set-piece; it is by this early sketch that Chaudhuri is represented in the new anthology of Indian writing in English edited by Salman Rushdie and Elizabeth West (Viking, 1997). I must admit that it was a revelation to me when I first read it, for in my own part of the country, in Uttar Pradesh, I had never known any town of its size which was even remotely so Westernized and, as I thought, so absurdly and pathetically imitative of dimly glimpsed Western culture. Above a door in a part of Chaudhuri's house, for example, there hung 'a coloured reproduction of Raphael's *Madonna della Sedia*' and all around could be found four other Western pictures one of which, Chaudhuri tells us, 'certainly was not by Greuze'—in case we were so ignorant or careless as to think it might have been! Unlike any other Indian author I can think of, Chaudhuri was thus virtually born knowing his Raphael from his Greuze—or certainly-not-Greuze—and even within Raphael, his *Madonna della Sedia* from the *Madonna della Granduca* from the *Madonna della Colonna* and each of these from the Madonna of the Meadow. Evidently, the iron of Westernization had entered the Bengali soul earlier and far deeper than it had Indian souls in other parts of the country, a circumstance which may help explain the seemingly ineradicable Anglophilia of educated Bengalis in general and Chaudhuri in particular. It also explains why Chaudhuri has consistently distinguished between Bengalis on the one hand and all other Indians including 'Hindustanis' (which in Bengali means mainly residents of the Hindi/Hindustani-speaking North India) on the other. In fact, if one were to sketch out a career graph of Chaudhuri as a writer, it would appear that in the first phase of his life spent in Bengal from 1897 to 1942, his main subject is his own formation as an educated Bengali; in the second phase spent in Delhi from 1942 to 1970, his grand theme is the present post-colonial or more accurately post-imperialist state of India; and in his latest and current phase, in which he has lived in Oxford since 1970, his subject has been, somewhat more remotely, the colonial past of India as well as the present decay of England.

II

Of the books which followed the *Autobiography, A Passage of England* (1959) and *The Continent of Circe* (1966) were also major works, in their own very different ways, and together constitute the triptych on which Chaudhuri's fame must rest. The Unknown Indian had become so well known for writing just that one book that it led to his fondest dream coming true: he was invited to England. It was a five-week visit, but so packed with the good things of life and so keenly enjoyed and observed by the fifty-seven year old Chaudhuri that it proved long enough for him to get a book out of it. The interplay between the England he had already known perhaps a little too much about at second hand, and the England which he now came briefly to observe and experience at first hand, forms one of the main points of interest in this voyage of discovery, and it is characteristic that even after he has been there, Chaudhuri says that the derivative England of books and prints which he had carried out him from India was ultimately the 'truer' one! The real post-imperialist England seemed to be in disarray and decay, and Chaudhuri preferred to hang on to his fond illusions of a pristine imaginary homeland.

Not that he saw nothing good in the real England around him. One of the finest insights he has ever achieved was to notice that England continued to look 'unreal' to him throughout his stay, not because of the psychological gap between expectation and reality but rather because of the material reason that he wasn't used to seeing things constantly in a grey and overcast perspective. Chaudhuri's description of the soft and cloudy English daylight, especially in contrast with the harsher tones of an Indian day, is one of the acutest pieces of physical description by him, and as nearly always with his physical observations, thereby hangs a theory. He calls it 'Meeting the Third Dimension', his argument being that while the 'fierce sun' of India 'disrupted architectural masses', the softer light in England gave everything a solidity, a third dimension. By now, of course, both the senses of the world 'vision' are beginning to converge, though Chaudhuri may not wish to admit it. If he felt that he had lived all his life in India until that advanced point only in two dimensions and became whole and entire only in England, it was not only because of the light; it was also because he had now attained his enlightenment. From now on, there would be no real peace for him until he could inhabit the Third Dimension permanently.

Meanwhile, he had another decade to spend in his old country, for which he now invented a metaphor even more comprehensively damning than V.S. Naipaul's *Area of Darkness.* Going back to an episode narrated in Homer's *Odyssey,* he called India the Continent of Circe, a land to which successive races had been enticed only to be turned into swine by the sorceress who ruled the land. He felt he had hit upon his grand theme here, for he promised a whole 'series' of works of this kind of which, however, only the one materialized. It remains a wide-angle sociological survey of India, based on a definitely eccentric and partial reading of history, much personal observation, and his own brand of fusty scholarship. It is, at the same time, a potent and pungent book, ever rambling and ramifying like all books by Chaudhuri, but packing more of a punch through its sheer intensity of personal conviction.

By now the Chaudhuri persona of a pugilistically polemical writer was well established. In fact, *Circe* made him probably the most controversial writer of that turbulent transformational decade, a decade of many national crises and a fair amount of soul-searching, the decade (as the Hindi word has it) of *moha-bhanga* or disenchantment with our independent nation-state and our two decades of freedom. But Chaudhuri wasn't really a part of this widely prevalent mood; he was, as always, his own man, even in his disillusionments. He wasn't concerned with the current affairs and problems of the nation; he wanted instead to offer an explanation for the whole miserable history of India, and he had a theory which accounted for it.

This theory is about as absurd as theories can be and shows Chaudhuri at is nuttiest and fruitiest best! It amounts briefly to the hypothesis that 'we Hindus' were originally Europeans but had been beguiled into coming to India where 'the tropical climate' had been our ruin and undoing. And the same pattern was repeated in the case of all comers to India, including lately the British. It wasn't anything human; it was the climate.

For a theory comparably preposterous, one may go to E.M. Forster's *A Passage to India*, a liberal novel which Chaudhuri detests despising in particular its Indian hero Aziz, while preferring instead *Kim* by that hard-core imperialist Kipling. In Forster, at the climactic trial scene, not content merely to narrate Aziz's alleged misdeed but striving also to account for it through a grand theory he has evolved of 'Oriental Pathology', the police superintendent MacBryde comes up with the notion that while the 'pinko-grey' races are not sexually attracted to the darker races, it is *vice versa* almost with a vengeance. Chaudhuri's theory seems equally arbitrary, except that it is based not on race but on the climate. (I am told by my friend Dr Roger Hooker that when he and his wife Pat once visited Nirad Chaudhuri in Delhi in the late 1960s, and when Mrs Hooker remarked to Chauduri that he seemed to be 'a geographical determinist', he agreed only too readily: 'Yes, yes, that's just what I am—a geographical determinist'!)

By now, Chaudhuri had begun to talk of his own 'quixotism', and more heroically, of himself as 'a lone critic of the rest of the three hundred million (Hindus), and the risks are all mine.' On the last page of *Circe*, his sense of estrangement with his own country and his own people became so acute as to be not only savage in the manner of Swift (whose category of the Yahoos he borrowed to describe his compatriots) but also outright misanthropic:

> But why should I concern myself with them? I have rescued my European soul (!) from Circe....I have recovered my Ariel's body from Sycorax.... So I can and should ignore the Yahoos. But I would save the fellow-beasts. They do not, however, listen to me. They honk, neigh, bellow, bleat, or grunt, and scamper away to their scrub, stable, byre, pen, and sty.

This abysmally sub-human vision of his fellow Indians indicated just one thing, that Chaudhuri himself was about to defect, to scamper away to greener and pleasanter pastures—or at least so they then seemed to him.

Chaudhuri was probably at the height of his fame in India in the late 1960s, in the wake of the controversy caused by *The Continent of Circe*. I recall that when I first came to Delhi in 1969 to begin teaching at St Stephen's College (where a colleague of mine, Dan O'Connor, knew Chaudhuri, visited him several times at his Mori Gate flat, and invited him to speak in college), all kinds of colourful and even comical rumours were afloat in the campus regarding Chaudhuri. One of these had it that whenever Chaudhuri came out of his house to walk down the mean lower-middle class street on which he lived near Mori Gate, street urchins would gather round attracted by his exotic dress of suit-boot-and-hat and would clap their hands and sing 'Johnny Walker! Johnny Walker!!' as they followed him. And, to rub it in, they did not even refer to the whisky; they meant the Bombay film comedian of that name, who too was often dressed in a suit and tie as he performed his farcical roles. (I always thought all this was somewhat exaggerated, until I found it confirmed in print by Chaudhuri himself in the *Continent of Circe*, where he even adds in an authenticating detail that those who surrounded and followed him jeered at him 'in a ribald manner', shouting after him in Hindi: '*Arrey Jahny*', i.e., O my sweetheart!)

III

When Chaudhuri reached England for a second time in June 1970, it was never to come back to India, not even for a short visit—at least not yet! As he was driven off from the airport in London to Oxford, he turned to his wife and said, 'I am feeling as if I was a soldier come home on leave from a battle-front.' But little did he know. As soon as he began earnestly to live in England, it too became a battle-field for him where he felt estranged from and entrenched against the society at large. The British withdrawal from India had been, Chaudhuri now realized, not only India's undoing; it was even more so England's. If India without England was drifting towards chaos, England after India was beginning to rot at the core. Whatever the facts of the case, what this meant was that Chaudhuri was (as a popular Urdu couplet has it) no happier in the garden than he had been in the cage. Why, given his temper, wherever he was was his battle-field.

The books which Chaudhuri produced after reaching England marked a great contrast from those he had been writing in India. The pen as the flaming sword seemed to have been replaced by the orientalist's quill, the inequities of the present by the curiosities of the past. Worse still, nearly all these books arose not from his own agitated breast but had been suggested to him by well-meaning others. The 'project' of writing a new biography of Friederich Max Mueller, *Scholar Extraordinary* (1974), had been proposed to him, as Chaudhuri acknowledged, 'by my friend Laurens van der Post', and the idea for his even less inspired biography *Clive of India* (1975) came to him from elsewhere as well. Even his *Hinduism* (1979), a book on a subject which had always been close if not dear to his heart, was the result of a publisher, Lord Weidenfeld, having asked him to contribute this volume to their series, *History of Religion,* even though he did not eventually publish it for the reason that Chaudhuri apparently failed to meet the deadline. But all these bespoken books suggest a man who had either lost his *metier* or was in his reduced circumstances (in a phrase and practice much prevalent in Victorian England) 'penny-a-lining.'

The one book from the last quarter-century which evokes the Chaudhuri of old is in fact a sequel, the second volume of his autobiography. At nearly a thousand pages, it is even longer than the *Unknown Indian* and no less lively and acute, though it is now distinctly less personal and rather more public and political, as indicated in the sub-title: *Thy Hand, Great Anarch!: India 1921-1952* (1987). It has the same felicity and insightfulness, though these qualities are perhaps naturally not as impressive as they were when first sighted in the *Unknown Indian*, and it has the same startling, absurd oddity of the narratorial character on display, in all innocence of its absurdity, as before. Indeed, the most priceless single gem of Chaudhuri's whole life (at least in my own subjective and possibly singular preference) is to be found in this volume. Here is Chaudhuri describing his wedding night, and his first tentative attempts to get to know his young bride who was 'a complete stranger' to him:

> I asked her timidly after a while: 'Have you listened to any European music?' She shook her head to say 'No'. Nonetheless I took another chance and this time asked: 'Have you heard the name of a man called Beethoven?' She nodded and signified 'Yes.' I was reassured, but not wholly satisfied. So I asked yet again: 'Can you spell the name?' She said slowly: 'B, E, E, T, H, O, V, E, N.' I felt very encouraged. After that we talked about other things aimlessly and dozed off.

If the so called East-West encounter has engendered a scene more intimately hilarious and pathetic at once, I do not know of it. The Hungarian humorist George Mikes observed some decades ago that while the rest of the world had sex, the English had hot water bottles. It would appear that the Anglicized Bengali *babu* went one better. Such was the Western spell cast on him that the correct spelling of odd Western names became for him the height of fulfilment, the consummation of bliss, the essence of *jouissance.* Incidentally, bizarre uses of Beethoven have not notably diminished in Anglophone India. In his recent novel *Beethoven Among the*

Cows (1995), Rukun Advani has Beethoven stand for all that is Western and civilized while the cows are of course all that is crass and Indian.

The dominant note of *Thy Hand*, however, is not private but public. Here too, Chaudhuri displays a marked oddity and limitation. As Subhash's brother Sarat Bose's private secretary for three and a half years (1937-41), he had the advantage of watching some of our national events and figures for some of the time from close quarters. Yet he cannot see Gandhi for his goats, Nehru for his Oxbridge bias and his English accent (such as these might have been), and even Subhash for his 'closed mind' as could be expected in the case of 'a typical Bengali intellectual'! Indeed, Chaudhuri shows here as elsewhere in his work his great gift for thinking and observing the worst of any person or situation, which naturally leads on to his bottomless pessimism. As the allusive title of this book indicates, Chaudhuri wishes to lay claim to his own share of the famous English 'Tory gloom' of the eighteenth century, as most memorably expressed by Alexander Pope and his friend Jonathan Swift. 'Thy hand, Great Anarch! lets the curtain fall;/And Universal Darkness buries all!' are the concluding lines of Pope's great mock-epic *The Dunciad* (1728/1742), and there can be little doubt that Chaudhuri sees the great galaxy of our nationalist leaders as no better than a set of blundering dunces, the more despicable in his eyes for leading India closer and closer to independence from Britain. Yet another source of unrelievable gloom for Chaudhuri might have been his location in the much declined and decayed Britain of the 1980s as he wrote this book which is ostensibly about India from the 1920s to the 1950s. One has a hunch that if Chaudhuri were to get round to writing yet another voluminous volume of his autobiography, describing his English years from 1970 upto date, his gloom would be even denser and more appalling. For that book will have to be about not the Continent of Circe and its wicked sorceress, but about the English God, the Gauranga Mahaprabhu (fair-skinned god), who failed—or at least failed Chaudhuri.

In comparison, 'Mr.Chaudhuri's new book' which he told me about as through a glass darkly and which as we all know now is titled *Three Horsemen of the New Apocalypse* (1997), is, at a mere 137 pages, no more than a splutter. When he told me about this book just before its publication, Chaudhuri claimed that it was a very 'different kind of a book,' for it had 'nothing to do with India and nothing to do with me.' That would have been a new kind of book for Chaudhuri indeed, for India and himself have constantly been his two grand themes, and perhaps not in that order either. But alas, this book is no such thing. The three horses of the title, which are individualism, nationalism and democracy, have been his *betes noire* or at least hobby horses for some time now, and the third and last part of the book, titled 'Decline and Fall of Western Civilization with its Worldwide Offshoots' and comprising chapters on 'Decadence of Western Civilization', 'Decadence of the English People', 'Decadence in India' and 'Decadence in the United States', will be no news even to casual Chaudhuri-watchers. For Chaudhuri, not ripeness but rottenness is all.

IV

Chaudhuri is a writer difficult to estimate. On the positive side is his extraordinarily long and unflagging career which began in January 1926 (as documented in a volume of his early journalistic pieces edited by his son Dhruva under the flagrantly ungrammatical title *The East is East and the West is West*, (1996) and which continues unabated three score and ten years later; those *Three Horsemen* should surely get him into the *Guinness Book of Records*. He has undeniably a gift for acute observation of both physical and social phenomena and for rendering his views in a cuttingly apt style. On top of that, he has even acuter self-awareness, a form of knowledge which he accepts and transmits equanimitously enough. For example, he has himself spoken of 'my sharp and biting tongue' and his gift from the start for 'making barbed observations.' 'The prevalent attitude towards Englishmen of our people,' he has stated, 'was one of irrational and ineradicable cringing and equally irrational and unconquerable hatred'—without in this instance indicating how far he is himself complicit in this ambivalent attitude. Finally, in the second volume of his autobiography, he even wonders whether the reader 'has been able to develop any compassion for me in spite of my follies.'

All this seems quite modest and fetching, until one remembers the prevalent tone and style of Chaudhuri's writing. Shakespeare was said to have 'small Latin and less Greek', and though Chaudhuri's own laboriously autodidactic stock of Latin and Greek and French and Italian—and for that matter Sanskrit—may not be considerably larger, he deploys it as if it were. Witness not the sub but the super-title of his *Continent of Circe*, which runs '*De rerum Indicarum natura: Exempla gentium et seditionum*', whatever that might mean, and witness too the concluding chapter of *Thy Hand* which bears the title '*Credo Ut Intelligam*' and ends with eight lines of untranslated French verse. As Shakespeare said of some of his own creations, it seems that Chaudhuri has been to a great feast of languages and picked up only the crumbs. Or, as Shakespeare also put it, Chaudhuri plays such stylistic tricks before high heavens as make the angels weep.

This is the more glaring because such pretentious swagger coexists with numerous delightful examples of apt and simple English. It is as if Chaudhuri were offering us not only himself but also, unconsciously, a cruel caricature of himself, as a writer hoist with his own petard. His extremely self-conscious regard for the value of style makes all this even worse. Even though *The New Statesman* had early declared that Chaudhuri 'writes like an angel' (which presumably is the next best thing to writing like a true-born Englishman!), Chaudhuri yet devised a means of further improving his English style. This, as he proclaimed in a lecture before the Royal Society of Literature on being made its fellow in 1979, was to begin eating like an Englishman. At a feeble and delicate five feet one, which is what he is, this seemed to him the best way of beefing up his style. 'O on what meat doth this our Caesar feed,' Shakespeare asked, 'That he hath grown so great?' The answer in the case of Nirad Babu would be: On beefsteak and Yorkshire pudding perhaps, washed down with something nicely appropriate.

In the last few years, however, Chaudhuri has surprised many readers by beginning to publish in Bengali while keeping presumably to the same non-Bengali diet. His flair for collective self-flagellation and self-excoriation seems to work even better in his own language, apparently, if we may judge by the titles of two of his Bengali books: *Atmaghati Bangali* and *Atmaghati Rabindranath* (i.e., The Self-destructive Bengalis, and The Self-destructive Tagore). The poet Shankho Ghosh made an obvious rejoinder when in the title of a review he referred to Chaudhuri's own *Atmaghati Manisha* (Self-destructive Intellect).

In returning to write in Bengali after a life-time of perfecting an English style, Chaudhuri has of course eminent predecessors. Bankim wrote in Bengali after making a false start through his first novel, *Rajmohan's Wife*, in English, while Michael Madhusudan Dutt's fascination with England was more sustained, as also perhaps were the originality and the sheer scope of his Bengali writings afterwards. But these are, after all, inept comparisons, for there is no prospect really in Chaudhuri's case of the English prodigal son coming home. The crusty, musty and fusty English he writes is truly 'Babu English', as he himself acknowledged in the *Continent of Circe*, even as he defended his style which was as deferential in its way as it was meant to be defiant:

> Here I shall only say, and I say it as one of the very last of the babus who picked up the gauntlet thrown down by the English, that if I write the kind of English I write, it is due partly at least to the ridicule of our English by the local British, high and low.

Chaudhuri is probably one of the very last of the Bengali *babus* in some other senses as well: as someone desperately keen to imbibe and internalize as much Englishness as possible which he of course values the far side of adulation, and as someone who is (in a sense of the word *babus* which is available in Bengali but not in English) a bit of a dandy and a fop, what with his hat and bow-tie and ruffled shirts.

In the end one emphasizes the crucial importance of Chaudhuri's hard won style because it shows the man himself; it enacts the whole stance of his gnarled Anglophile leanings. In fact, in his very last i.e. latest book, *Three Horsemen*, Chaudhuri himself has gone further in this regard to coin a new *dictum*: 'Instead of saying that *le style est l'homme meme*, I say *le style est le sujet meme*.' It must be, when the man is his own grand subject

It used to be said, in the 1920s and for a while afterwards, that when good Americans died they went to Paris. There can similarly be no doubting that when a good Bengali *babu*, so to say, expires, he even now ascends to Oxford. Except that in Nirad Chaudhuri's case, while he himself gloriously lives on, it is good old Oxford which has died on his hands, as has the rest of England, which lies putrescent all around. Though he has surely gone there, the Heaven of Englishness is not what it used to be, or what Chaudhuri, the last and by no means least of the Bengali *babus*, fondly imagined it to be.

NOTES ON THE CONTRIBUTORS

Basu, Shrabani : was born on 15 August 1962. She studied at St. Stephen's College, Delhi University. She began her career as a trainee journalist at *The Times of India*, 1983 and is presently the Anand Bazar Group's London correspondent writing for most of their publications including the *Ananda Bazar Patrika*, *Sunday Magazine* and *The Telegraph*. She has covered a vast spectrum of subjects from Indo-British relations to stories on Sikh and Kashmiri separatists working from London. Her stories on Nirad Chaudhuri invariably invited a flood of letters from angry Bengalis as he nearly always said something controversial.

Bose, Krishna : is an eminent writer, educationist and parliamentarian. She taught at the City College of Calcutta where she was also Head of the English Department and Principal for a few years. Her published works include *Itihaser Santhane*, Ananda, Calcutta, 1982; *Charanarekha Taba*, Ananda, Calcutta, 1992; *1947: Smriti Bismriti*, Ananda, Calcutta,1982; *Prasanga Subhaschandra*, Ananda, Calcutta, 1992; *Netaji: A Biography for the Young*, Rupa, Delhi, 1995; and *Ek Namber Bari*, Ananda, Calcutta, 1997. She is a member of the governing body of the Institute of Child Health, Calcutta and the Council of the Netaji Research Bureau, and the president of Vivek Chetana—a non-profit organization for disadvantaged women and children. She is also an accomplished classical musician.

Daruwalla, Keki : is a distinguished poet. His published works include *Under Orion* (1970), *Landscapes*, (1987), *Winter Poems*, *A Summer of Tigers*, (1995), and *The Minister for Permanent Unrest*, (1997). In 1984 he was awarded the Sahitya Academy Award and the Commonwealth Poetry Prize (Asia Region) in 1987 for *Landscapes*. He has spent a year at Oxford as a Visiting Fellow under the Colombo Plan.

Dev Sen, Nabaneeta : is Professor and former Chair at the Department of Comparative Literature, Jadavpur University, Calcutta.

A student of Harvard University (USA), Indiana University (USA), Presidency College and Jadavpur University (Calcutta), Dev Sen has a Masters degree in English and another in Comparative Literature and a Doctorate in the latter. At the moment she is the Radhakrishnan Fellow at Oxford University, besides being a Fellow of the Royal Asiatic Society and member of several international bodies of literature and semiotics.

Dev Sen is a leading poet and writer in Bengali, with about forty published books of fiction, travelogues and poems.

Jack, Ian Grant : was born on 7 February 1945. He was educated at Dunfermline High School, Fife. Beginning his career as a trainee journalist with *Glasgow Herald* in 1965 he has worked as a reporter for *Cambuslang Advertiser* and *East Kilbride News* (1966), as a journalist for Scottish Daily Express (1966-77), *Sunday Times* (1970-86) *Observer* and *Vanity Fair* (NY) (1986-88). In 1989, he became the Deputy Editor and in 1991, the Executive Editor of *Independent on Sunday.* He was awarded Journalist of the Year and Granada TV What The Papers Say Award (1985), Colour Magazine Writer of the Year (1985), Reporter of the Year (1988), British Press Awards and National Newspaper Editor of the Year (1985), and the Newspaper Form Awards (1992). His published works include *Before the Oil Ran Out* (1987). Ian Jack enjoys travel, reading on the imperial history of India and steamships. Presently, he is the editor of *Granta.*

Malik, Amita : author, columnist, feature writer and broadcaster, Amita Malik was born and grew up in Assam. She has specialized in writing about culture, the arts and the media. Her weekly columns are among the most widely read in India. A gold medalist in English twice over from Calcutta University, Amita Malik is also the only woman to have won India's most prized journalistic award, the B.D. Goenka Award for Excellence in Journalism in 1994. Her books include *The Year of The Vulture,* a documented account of the atrocities committed in Bangladesh during its fight for freedom, and *India Watching,* a study of the Indian image on foreign media in fourteen countries, written under the auspices of The Indian Institute of Advanced Study. Widely travelled, having served on several international and national juries for films and TV, Amita Malik lives in Delhi and her hobbies are hill driving, dogs and gourmet cooking.

Mukherjee Meenakshi : is a professor of English at the Jawaharlal Nehru University, New Delhi. She has also worked as visiting faculty in University of Chicago, University of Texas at Austin, University of California at Berkeley, New York State University, Macquire University at Sydney, Flinders University at Adelaide, University of Canberrra. She is also Fellow at the Rockefeller Centre at Bellagio, Italy. Her publications include *The Twice Born Fiction Themes and Techniques in Indian Novels in English*, Heinemann, London and Delhi, 1974; *Realism and Reality: Novel and Society in India*, Oxford University Press, New Delhi, 1985; *Jane Austen, Women Writer's Series*, Macmillan, London, 1991, reprinted in India as *Rereading Jane Austen*, Orient Longman, 1995; *Let's Go Home and Other Stories*, Orient Longman, Madras, 1974; *Critical Edition of Rajmohan's Wife* (the first Indian novel in English) Ravi Dayal Publishers, New Delhi, 1996; *The Naked King and Other Poems* by Nirendranath Chakrabarty, (tr. from Bengali with Sujit Mukherjee) Writer's Workshop, Calcutta 1974; *The Virgin of Babughat* (tr. from the Bengali novel by Lokenath Bhattacharya).

Radice, William : is a well-known Tagore scholar and translator. He has also translated Martin Kåmpchen's *The Honey-Seller and Other Stories* from the German to English, and edited Juan Mascaro's *The Creation of Faith*. Presently, he teaches at the School of Oriental and African Studies, London.

Singh, K. Natwar- : was born in 1930. He was educated at Mayo College, Ajmer, Scindia School, Gwalior, St. Stephen's College, Delhi, and Corpus Cristi, Cambridge. He joined the Indian Foreign Service in 1953 and has served as Ambassador to Poland and Pakistan, and High Commissioner to Namibia. In the course of his career he has also served in Beijing, London, New York; in the Prime Minister's Secretariat (1966-71); as Secretary General 7th NAM Summit; Chief Coordinator, Commonwealth Summit, (1983). In 1984 he was awarded the Padma Bhushan, elected President of the Delhi Gymkhana Club, elected to Lok Sabha, and served as Union Minister of State for Steel and Fertilizers and External

Affairs (1984-89). He was elected President, UN Conference of Disarmament and Development (1987), President of All India Tennis Federation (1988-92), leader of the Indian Delegation to 42nd Session of the General Assembly of the UN (1987). His publications include ed. *E. M. Forster: A Tribute*, New York, 1964; ed. *The Legacy of Nehru*, New York, 1963; ed. *Tales from Modern India*, New York, 1966; *Maharaja Surajmal*, London, 1981; *Curtain Raisers*, New Delhi, 1984.

Singh, Khushwant : is one of India's best-known columnists and journalists. He has had a chequered career. Educated at Government College, Lahore and at King's College and the Inner Temple in London, he practised at the Lahore High Court for several years before joining the Ministry of External Affairs in 1947. He was sent on diplomatic posting to Canada and London. He began his career as a journalist with All India Radio in 1951. From 1969-79, he edited the *Illustrated Weekly of India*, going on to become editor of *The Hindustan Times* from 1980-83. He is also the author of several books including a classic two-volume history of the Sikhs and a number of translated works. His novels include *Delhi* and *Train to Pakistan* which won the Grove Press Award for the best work of fiction in 1954. He was a Member of Parliament from 1980-86.

Trivedi, Harish : is professor and Head of the English Department at the Delhi University. He has also taught at Allahabad University and at St. Stephen's, Delhi, and has been a visiting scholar/fellow at the universities of Wales, Birmingham and Georgia. His published works include *Colonial Transactions: English Literature and India,* Calcutta, 1993; Manchester & New York, 1995, as well as numerous articles on English, American and Indian Literatures, translations of poetry, fiction and biography from Hindi to English. He has also co-edited *Interrogating Post-colonialism,* Simla.

BIBLIOGRAPHY

English

1.	The Autobiography of An Unknown Indian	1951
2.	A Passage to England	1959
3.	The Continent of Circe	1965
4.	The Intellectual in India	1967
5.	To Live or Not to Live	1971
6.	Scholar Extraordinary	1974
7.	Clive of India	1975
8.	Culture in the Vanity Bag	1976
9.	Hinduism	1979
10.	Thy Hand, Great Anarch!	1987
11.	The East is East and The West is West	1996
12.	Three Horsemen of the New Apocalypse	1997
13.	From the Archives of A Centenarian	1997

Bengali

1.	Bangali Jeebane Ramoni	1968
2.	Atmaghati Bangali	1988
3.	Atmaghati Rabindranath – I	1992
4.	Amar Devatwar Sampatti	1994
5.	Atmaghati Rabindranath – II	1996
6.	Amar Desh Amar Shatak	1996